HOW TO READ
SKYSCRAPERS

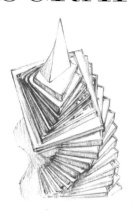

HOW TO READ
SKYSCRAPERS

A crash course in high-rise architecture

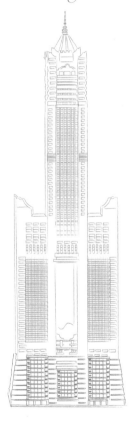

IVY PRESS

Edward Denison
& Nick Beech

This edition published in the UK in 2019 by
Ivy Press
An imprint of The Quarto Group
The Old Brewery, 6 Blundell Street
London N7 9BH, United Kingdom
T (0)20 7700 6700 F (0)20 7700 8066
www.QuartoKnows.com

First published in the UK in 2019

© 2019 Quarto Publishing plc

British Library Cataloguing-in-Publication Data
A catalogue record for this book is available from
the British Library

ISBN: 978-1-78240-649-5

This book was conceived, designed and produced by
Ivy Press
58 West Street, Brighton BN1 2RA, UK

PUBLISHER Susan Kelly
EDITORIAL DIRECTOR Tom Kitch
ART DIRECTOR James Lawrence
EDITORS Stephanie Evans, Angela Koo
DESIGN JC Lanaway
ILLUSTRATORS Adam Hook, Sarah Skeate
EDITORIAL ASSISTANT Niamh Jones

Printed in China

10 9 8 7 6 5 4 3 2 1

Contents

Nearly 3,000 years ago, the Assyrian king Sennacherib boasted of building walls "as high as mountains" when transforming the city of Nineveh into the largest city in the world. Despite the renown of these monumental fortifications, their height paled in comparison to the Great Pyramid of Giza, erected almost 2,000 years earlier during the reign of a similarly absolute ruler, Pharaoh Khufu. Khufu's tomb remained the tallest artificial structure for more than 3,800 years until the construction of the cathedral spire in Lincoln, UK, from the late twelfth century. In the subsequent centuries, the world's tallest structures were testament to the uniquely human belief in spiritual authority, a belief that began to wane at the dawn of The Enlightenment and the irrepressible march of science, technology and commerce. Today, these same forces have resulted in buildings that would far surpass the imagination of ancient pharaohs, kings, and priests.

Yet, whether for posterity, defense, worship, business, or pleasure, every skyscraping structure ever constructed shares the common dependence on the combination of a concentrated wealth and power of a few, the speciality knowledge of experts, and the labor of many. When humankind's concerns were directed toward the earthly powers of kings and spiritual powers of gods, the tallest buildings were necessarily directed and delivered by the State and Church. Since the Enlightenment, the market—whether in the shape of powerful private individuals or corporations—has been just as probable to possess the wealth and will to build tall.

These powerful interests today have access to technologies and knowledge far beyond that possessed by the

Medieval marvel
On completion of the central spire in 1311, Lincoln Cathedral was 525 feet (160 m) high. The cathedral was the world's tallest building until its spire collapsed in 1548.

ancients and peoples of the Middle Ages. Stone, wood, and clay, and the arts of stereotomy, have given way to iron, steel, concrete, and glass, and the science of structural engineering. But prior to the modern age, the civilizations of Europe, Africa, Asia, and the Americas were able to create buildings of heights that first matched and then surpassed the monuments of the ancient world. Through unique forms of trade, bureaucracy, and social order, highly skilled stonemasons and carpenters erected vastly complex towers.

The organization of labor and professions in modernity have resulted in an extraordinary development of the construction industry. Mechanized mass production, digital design and procurement tools, robotics, new materials, and a global workforce have led to unparalleled building proficiency. The modern skyscraper is little more than a century old, yet it has in its lifetime more than quadrupled in height, putting the long-fabled milestone of a kilometer—or 3,280 feet—tall now literally and firmly within reach.

INTRODUCTION

But it is not only "height" that marks the advance of the skyscraper. The modern skyscraper has come to represent the flowering of particular cultures in the twentieth century—particularly in North America—and subsequently the new global cities of the Pacific, Indian Ocean, and Middle East. Being a symbol of commerce in the present as well as a vision of the future, the esthetics of the skyscraper often reveal the ideologies and motivations of clients and designers. At the same time, the skyscraper is marked by environmental concerns.

Situated in landscapes that may be prone to earthquakes, extreme temperatures and weather, or rising sea levels, modern engineers have sought to stabilize and secure the skyscraper as a structure, resulting at times in extraordinary forms. Similarly, the need to reduce carbon emissions under the threat of global warming has resulted in ingenious heating, cooling, lighting, and even new ecological systems. Skyscrapers have by their very nature constantly challenged the established practices of the myriad professions engaged

in their design and construction. Through extraordinary ingenuity and innovation, these buildings have transformed most cities on the earth and have become one of the quintessential images of urban and architectural aspiration.

This book charts the history of humankind's desire to build tall through the structures and buildings that exemplify this compulsion throughout the ages and across the world. The intention is not to provide a catalog of the biggest and the best, but instead to reveal the more complex history of skyscrapers globally. This book is not, therefore, merely a guide to reading the buildings themselves through their histories, innovations, and characteristics, but an attempt to provide a reading of the genre and how it impacted different places, cultures, and professions throughout time.

Soaring ever higher
Urban necessities or arrogant follies, the passion for building tall—and megatall—has defined the skyline of cities on almost every continent.

Introduction

Stonehenge, UK

With the passing of time, the origins of ancient monuments were lost. New civilizations found it difficult to comprehend how massive structures, such as Stonehenge in southwest England, which was erected in ca. 2,500 BCE, were built, let alone for what purpose. Frequently, the explanation was mythic—giants, wizards, or gods must have produced such tall edifices.

For thousands of years, long before the skyscrapers of the modern world, humans have built upward, desiring to look down on the earth from above. Pharaohs and priests sought to cement their authority in the cosmic order. Later religious buildings reached upward, not to storm the heavenly, but to reflect its majesty. Tall buildings often had practical, secular ends, too. Commanding the landscape had military benefits, while height proved protection against natural forces and enabled the study of nature.

What makes a "skyscraper" can also change with perspective. A person from Chicago or Tokyo may look at the ruins of a Roman bath house in Great Britain and shrug. But when the Anglo-Saxons of the tenth century discovered those ruins in the undergrowth,

they found them so awesome to behold that they were ascribed to giants. But in fact those ancient monuments were the product of practical human actions. Utilizing wood, clay, stone, and iron, builders of the past created monuments that have stood into our own day. Ancient monuments were the product of the most advanced technologies of their time. Levers, ramps, pulleys, razor-sharp cutting tools, highly organized and skilled craftspeople, and armies of labor were combined and directed to create these cultural wonders.

Beginning this book on skyscrapers with the history of ancient tall buildings, we get more than just a pre-history. Examining these monuments reveals the broad range of motivations for building tall, which still drive many of our skyscraper projects today.

Tower of Babel

Many mythologies in the world describe structures that are designed to link heaven and the earth. Perhaps the most enduring, however, relates to hubris—building tall, fueled by a desire to emulate and even storm heaven, as a path to destruction. The Tower of Babel, as described in the Book of Genesis (11:4) is built by the first people—who speak only one language—"Come, let us build ourselves a city, and a tower with its top in the heavens, and let us make a name for ourselves; otherwise we shall be scattered abroad upon the face of the whole earth." God, displeased, confounds the builders by preventing them from understanding one another, the tower collapses, and the people are scattered just as they had feared.

The tower in art

The Tower of Babel endures in European Judeo-Christian culture. This painting (one of two) by Pieter Bruegel the Elder (1563) is recognizable to many and remains fascinating for its architectural precision—Bruegel represents a realistic Roman architecture and engineering process. He also shows how such a building might begin to collapse.

Reaching for the moon (below)

Inspired by Bruegel's painting, the Jesuit priest and scholar Athanasius Kircher (1602–80) analyzed the Tower of Babel—what if it really were attempted? Assuming the orbit of the moon as the horizon of "heaven," Kircher showed the impossibility of such a tower—the earth could not provide the bricks, the men, or the time.

The Confusion of Tongues (above)

The engraver Gustave Doré based his 1865 vision of the Tower of Babel on the minaret of the Great Mosque of al-Mutawakkil, in Samarra, Iraq. In reality, the minaret, or Malwiya Tower, was built in ca. 848–52 BCE, and reaches a height of 170 feet (52 m). It was partially destroyed in the thirteenth century by Hulagu Khan (grandson of Genghis Khan) and the minaret was damaged by a bomb in 2005.

Etemenanki

From the beginning of the twentieth century, archaeologists have identified the sixth-century BCE ziggurat of the ancient city of Babylon as the basis for the mythological Tower of Babel. Dedicated to Marduk, the Babylonian god, the "Temple of the Foundation of Heaven and Earth" (Etemenanki) is described in surviving cuneiform texts. These provide the dimensions for a tower at the center of the now-lost city.

Great Pyramids of Egypt

Standing giants
Completely dominating the landscape, the Great Pyramid of Giza was once clad in polished white limestone casing stones that would have reflected the sun. What remains is the stepped core. At its base, each side of the pyramid is 756 feet (230 m) long, and in volume the structure is more than 91 million cubic feet (almost 2.6 million m³).

In the fourth century BCE, a number of ancient Greeks began to record "wonders" or "sights to be seen" in the known world. Of the "Seven Wonders of the World" they described, only one still remains: the Great Pyramid of Giza. Also known as the Pyramid of Khufu (or Cheops in Hellenized or ancient Greek form)—after the pharaoh for whom it was built, the Great Pyramid is the oldest (constructed ca. 2560 BCE) and largest of six pyramids on the Giza plateau. Pyramids were created in ancient Egypt as tombs to encase the powerful pharaohs (some of whom were accepted as divine beings) and their retinue (including their wives and household—even their pets). At 481 feet (147 m), the Great Pyramid remained the tallest man-made structure in the world for more than 3,800 years.

Construction methods (left)

How the pyramids were constructed remains unknown. Archaeology at the Great Pyramid itself, at other pyramids, and at quarries and other related sites, combined with experimentation, and reconstructing possible building methods, suggests that the pyramid was built by skilled workers, who were quarrying with copper alloy picks, lifting coarse granite boulders from the surface, and dressing these using a combination of blade and sand.

Internal passages (right)

An interior passageway leads from a doorway near the base of the pyramid toward a subterranean chamber. An ascending passage splits into two paths—one develops into the Grand Gallery and reaches the King's Chamber, the other leads to the Queen's Chamber. Shafts leading from the chambers to the surface of the pyramid are oriented to the stars (Orion and north pole stars).

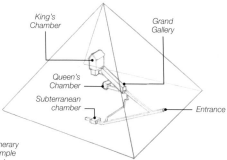

King's Chamber
Grand Gallery
Queen's Chamber
Subterranean chamber
Entrance

Tomb of Hemon
Pyramid of Khufu
Funerary temple
Pyramid of Khafre
Funerary temple of Khafre
Great Sphinx
Subsidiary pyramid
Mastabas and rock cut tombs
Valley of Kings
Pyramid of Menkaure
Funerary temple
Temple of Menkaure
Pyramid of Queens

Pyramid complex (left)

The Great Pyramid of Khufu is the largest of six pyramids at Giza. This, the Pyramid of Khafre (ca. 2558 BCE), and the relatively diminutive Pyramid of Menkaure (ca. 2510 BCE), are joined by a complex of smaller pyramids, tombs, and temples, along with the Great Sphinx (probably contemporary with the Pyramid of Khafre), forming a royal necropolis.

Pyramid of the Sun

A pyramid undressed
The pyramid was constructed in two phases some time in the first or second century CE; what can be seen today was completed in the first phase. The second phase brought its height to 264 feet (80 m). The completed pyramid was surmounted by an altar, which has not survived. Neither has the original limestone coating that was painted with colorful depictions of deities. The pyramid was also embellished with alabaster sculptures.

In the fourteenth century, the Tenochca (Aztec) people entered the Valley of Mexico and discovered a vast city in ruins containing a mighty pyramid structure. The Tenochca called this city Teotihuacán, and its main structure the Pyramid of the Sun. They believed it had been built by the gods and formed the origin of cosmic creation. In fact, they had discovered the ruined city of an ancient civilization that flourished between 100 BCE and 650 CE. Little is known about the cause of the fall of the people of Teotihuacán; the purpose of the Pyramid of the Sun remains unclear and its construction, too, is shrouded in mystery. At 216 feet (66 m), the surviving pyramid is less than half the height of the Great Pyramid of Giza (see page 14), but is one of the tallest ancient structures in the western hemisphere.

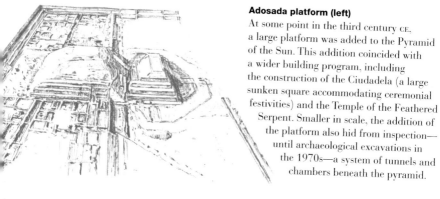

Adosada platform (left)

At some point in the third century CE, a large platform was added to the Pyramid of the Sun. This addition coincided with a wider building program, including the construction of the Ciudadela (a large sunken square accommodating ceremonial festivities) and the Temple of the Feathered Serpent. Smaller in scale, the addition of the platform also hid from inspection—until archaeological excavations in the 1970s—a system of tunnels and chambers beneath the pyramid.

Pyramids with a purpose? (right)

Unlike the Pyramids of Giza, the purpose of the Pyramid of the Sun, its sister the Pyramid of the Moon, or the later Pyramid of the Feathered Serpent, is unconfirmed. Though bodies, chambers (originally thought to be natural caves), masks, and other precious objects have all been discovered, no one knows why these items were contained in the pyramid.

Noguera Tunnel 1933

Smith Tunnel 1962

Gamio Tunnel 1920

Chamber

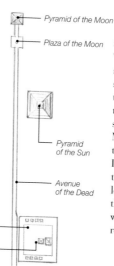

Pyramid of the Moon

Plaza of the Moon

Pyramid of the Sun

Avenue of the Dead

Ciudadela

Pyramid of the Feathered Serpent

Site map (left)

The plan of Teotihuacán suggests that despite its significance, the Pyramid of the Sun may not have been the city's focal point. The smaller Pyramid of the Moon dominates, because it terminates the Avenue of the Dead. The later Pyramid of the Feathered Serpent is located in direct relation to the Ciudadela (the Spanish word for "citadel"), the religious and political center.

Porcelain Pagoda

location: *Nanjing, China*

completed: *Fifteenth century*

In 1654, Johan Nieuhof, an envoy of the Dutch East India Company, visited China, recording the buildings and material culture he encountered. He describes a medieval "Wonder of the World"—a giant pagoda reaching 256 feet (78 m) into the sky, covered in brightly glazed porcelain, shimmering in the light of day, glittering with 100 lanterns at night, and jingling with hundreds of bells suspended from its corners. The Porcelain Pagoda, built in the fifteenth century, became famous throughout the world, was copied by architects, such as William Chambers in Great Britain, and recounted in fairy tales by writers, such as Hans Christian Anderson. It was destroyed in the nineteenth century; the pagoda seen today in Nanjing is a replica built in 2010, made from steel and glass.

Sacred structure

Traditionally, Chinese pagodas were built as sacred sites to house sacred relics and writings. The basic structure of this one was a nine-story octagonal frame, covered by glazed porcelain bricks and capped with a golden orb in the shape of a pineapple. A spiral staircase of 184 steps took visitors to the highest man-made point in China.

Liaodi Pagoda

Each story has doors on four sides and false windows on the other four sides

As with many pagodas, the Porcelain Pagoda was part of a wider temple complex. It may have been the most spectacular of its time, but the Porcelain Pagoda was far from the tallest. The Liaodi Pagoda, built of brick in 1055 CE, still stands at 276 feet (84 m), while the Tianning Temple Pagoda, built of wood between 2002 and 2007, at 505 feet (154 m), is now the tallest pagoda in the world.

Only the second story has a balcony

Liaodi means "Watching for the Enemy"—the original purpose of the tower

Master craftwork (above)

The white tiles for the Porcelain Pagoda were manufactured in Zhushan, Jingdezhen, in Jiangxi province. The bricks produced were remarkable for their size and intricacy. It is no longer possible—the skills and knowledge are lost—to produce porcelain with the thickness, detail, and quality of the original. The rich symbolic imagery in green, brown, and yellow, depicted sacred animals and deities.

Kew Gardens pagoda

William Chambers was just one of many eighteenth-century European architects to become interested in Chinese architecture. Employed by the Swedish East India Company, he traveled through China making studies and drawings of Chinese buildings, technology, and material culture. He designed a pagoda for London's royal botanical gardens based on his observations of the Nanjing Porcelain Pavilion.

Cologne Cathedral

location: *Cologne, Germany*

completed: *1880*

Heavenly heights
To this day, the cathedral towers over the city of Cologne. It is a shining example of European Gothic architecture, demonstrating the mastery of medieval stonemasons.

Begun in 1248, Cologne Cathedral in modern Germany is exceptional, a masterpiece of Gothic design that took more than 600 years to complete—it was only finished in 1880. Work was halted in 1473 and did not resume until the 1840s, although the original medieval plan, drawn on parchment, was adhered to throughout that long history. With the completion of its two great towers in 1880, the cathedral stood at 516 feet (157 m), and became the tallest building in the world. It was named a World Heritage Site by UNESCO in 1996.

Flying buttresses (below)

Instead of building increasingly thicker and heavier walls to support massive vaults, medieval masons used stone piers known as "flying buttresses."

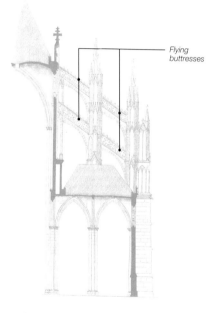

Flying buttresses

Soaring nave

At 142 feet (43 m) the nave of Cologne Cathedral is short of being the highest in the world by only 16 feet (5 m). But it has the highest height to width ratio of any nave, producing this impressive, soaring interior space.

Survival

Cologne Cathedral has been seriously damaged a number of times in history. It was occupied by the French Revolutionary Army in 1796, who used it as a storage and detention center. During World War II, the building was repeatedly bombarded and fire bombed. Remarkably, the building withstood all.

St. Peter's Basilica

Bramante's dome

An earlier hemispherical design for the dome of St. Peter's was made by Bramante more than 40 years before Michelangelo's, as reproduced in a 1905 drawing by Sebastiano Serlio. Bramante used the Roman Pantheon as inspiration in part because he had rediscovered a lost recipe for concrete.

One of the great spectacles from Renaissance Rome, St. Peter's Basilica—and in particular its main dome—was one of the tallest buildings of its time, reaching 448 feet (137 m). Initiated in 1505 by Pope Julius II, the construction of the Basilica involved the demolition of Old St. Peter's Basilica, a modest building dating from the fourth century CE. An ambitious building design by Donato Bramante, it included a concrete dome modeled on the Roman Pantheon. It took successive popes and their architects more than a hundred years to complete.

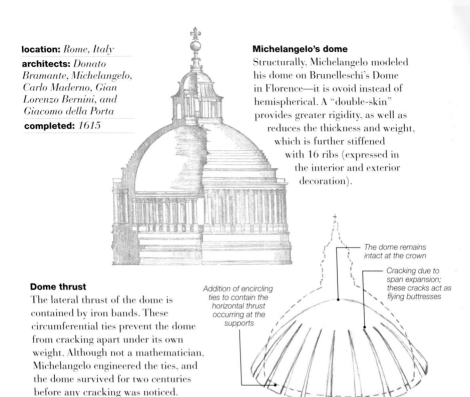

location: *Rome, Italy*

architects: *Donato Bramante, Michelangelo, Carlo Maderno, Gian Lorenzo Bernini, and Giacomo della Porta*

completed: *1615*

Michelangelo's dome

Structurally, Michelangelo modeled his dome on Brunelleschi's Dome in Florence—it is ovoid instead of hemispherical. A "double-skin" provides greater rigidity, as well as reduces the thickness and weight, which is further stiffened with 16 ribs (expressed in the interior and exterior decoration).

The dome remains intact at the crown

Cracking due to span expansion; these cracks act as flying buttresses

Addition of encircling ties to contain the horizontal thrust occurring at the supports

Dome thrust

The lateral thrust of the dome is contained by iron bands. These circumferential ties prevent the dome from cracking apart under its own weight. Although not a mathematician, Michelangelo engineered the ties, and the dome survived for two centuries before any cracking was noticed.

Dome interior

The dome of St. Peter's was begun by Michelangelo in 1547 and completed by Giacomo della Porta in 1590. It rests on four massive piers designed by Bramante. The dome is decorated with mosaics. The four evangelists are depicted in the spandrels, with the dome itself depicting papal figures and a heavenly host.

Leaning Tower of Pisa

location: *Pisa, Italy*

architects: *Bonanno Pisano, Gherardo di Gherardo (phase 1), Giovanni Pisano and Giovanni di Simone (phase 2)*

completed: *1399*

The Leaning Tower of Pisa was never the world's tallest tower, but it is one of the most remarkable, and most recognizable. Its unique quality is a result of bad engineering. Construction began in 1173, and one side began to sink as early as 1178, with just three stories built. Its lean was due to subsidence, a consequence of building an inadequate foundation—less than 10 feet (3 m) deep—in unstable ground. Work was hampered by wars, debt, and attempts to correct the lean. The delays allowed for the subsoil to compress, which is why the tower could be completed without toppling.

The Torre Pendente di Pisa

Pisa's tower was built in a Romanesque style, adapting classical Roman column and arch motifs to the bell tower typology. Originally it was intended to serve as a freestanding bell tower to the cathedral.

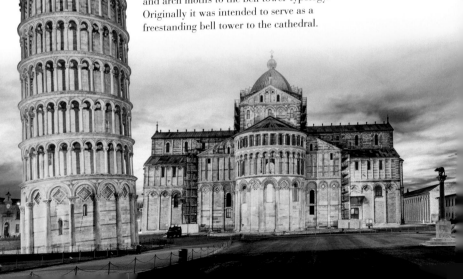

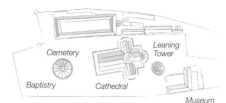

Square of Miracles

In the early eleventh century, Pisa was locked in ongoing conflict with neighboring cities Genoa, Lucca, and Florence. To assert its dominance, Pisa decided to construct a complex (the Piazza dei Miracoli, or Square of Miracles), which includes the Cathedral of Pisa, the Baptistry, and the Leaning Tower itself.

Bell chamber (above)

At the end of the twelfth century, having reached only the third story, construction ceased as a result of war with neighboring cities. Sporadic rebuilding continued up to 1272, with the appointment of Giovanni di Simone. The seventh story was added in 1319, and, finally, the bell chamber (with seven bells) in 1372, by Tommaso di Andrea Pisano. The bells were, apparently never rung, in fear that it would add to the stress on the Leaning Tower.

Fluctuating incline (below)

The tower is seven stories, and was built in just under 200 years. As stories were added, the lean of the tower increased. At one stage, it leaned at a 5.5-degree angle. Simone attempted to compensate for the lean by erecting a higher southern side. However, the extra weight exacerbated the subsidence problem—and increased the lean. As a result the tower has a slight banana curve.

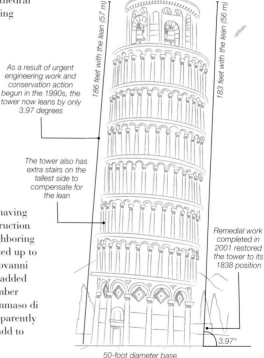

Original height on completion: 197 feet (60 m)

186 feet with the lean (57 m)

183 feet with the lean (56 m)

As a result of urgent engineering work and conservation action begun in the 1990s, the tower now leans by only 3.97 degrees

The tower also has extra stairs on the tallest side to compensate for the lean

Remedial work completed in 2001 restored the tower to its 1838 position

3.97°

50-foot diameter base

Two Towers of Bologna

location: *Bologna, Italy*
completed: *ca. 1116*

In the Middle Ages, the Italian city of Bologna was filled with towers. Built by wealthy merchant families at a time when assassination and murder were commonplace, each tower was both a symbol of wealth and a military stronghold. The most famous towers to remain standing are the so-called "Two Towers" of Asinelli (318 feet/97 m) and Garisenda (157 feet/48 m) originally built ca. 1109–1116, named after two competing families. These towers inspired the American architect Minoru Yamasaki in the design of the World Trade Center (see page 164).

Leaning towers
Both towers lean—the Garisenda more so. Originally both towers were of equal height (about 197 feet/60 m), but when extensions were attempted in the fourteenth century, the Garisenda was evidently weaker and it was "cut" to its present height; it lacks the castellated crown of the Asinelli.

Stone cores (right)

The stone towers are the remaining "cores" of wooden fortifications. The towers are made of selenite—the walls are thicker and heavier at the base, lighter at the summit. They rest on wooden stilts hammered into the ground and capped with pebble and lime. Originally, these would have wrapped around the towers. It is believed that Giovanni Visconti, Duke and Archbishop of Milan, constructed a fort that bridged the two towers to suppress the people of Bologna.

Medieval skyline

Many Italian towns developed peculiar skylines in the medieval period. Competition and open warfare between rival families resulted in a forest of towers in each town.

Garisenda

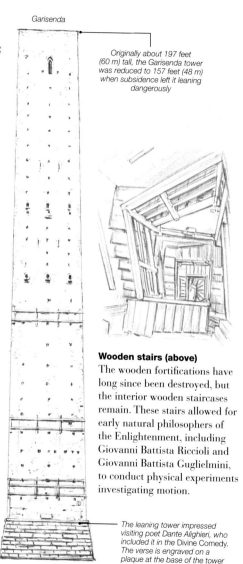

Originally about 197 feet (60 m) tall, the Garisenda tower was reduced to 157 feet (48 m) when subsidence left it leaning dangerously

Wooden stairs (above)

The wooden fortifications have long since been destroyed, but the interior wooden staircases remain. These stairs allowed for early natural philosophers of the Enlightenment, including Giovanni Battista Riccioli and Giovanni Battista Guglielmini, to conduct physical experiments investigating motion.

The leaning tower impressed visiting poet Dante Alighieri, who included it in the Divine Comedy. The verse is engraved on a plaque at the base of the tower

The Donjon of Château de Coucy

location: *Picardy, France*
completed: *Thirteenth century*

Castles were the most advanced form of military technology in the middle ages. By the thirteenth century two fundamental elements in castle design had reached their zenith—the high crenellated "curtain wall," and even higher stone towers. The design of towers had evolved from square to polygonal to circular in response to defensive requirements. The Donjon (the castle keep) of the Château de Coucy, built in the 1220s by Enguerrand III, Lord of Coucy, was Europe's largest, standing at 180 feet (55 m).

Prominent presence
The Donjon of Château de Coucy dominated the landscape around it. Built on a spur over the river and valley of Ailette, the Donjon was not only defensively secure, it was aesthetically dominant. The tower could be seen for 6 miles (10 km) in every direction.

Simple structure (right)

The Donjon consists of only three stories—each story measured close to 50 feet (15 m) in height (equivalent to about five apartments). Each story contained a hexagonal rib vault, and the walls were cut with arrow slits.

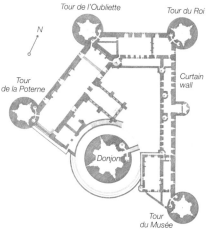

Tour de l'Oubliette

Tour du Roi

N

Tour de la Poterne

Curtain wall

Donjon

Tour du Musée

Group of towers (left)

The Donjon was one of five towers ("*tours*")—the four others, although smaller, were still huge. All the towers were cylindrical—these could hold their structure better than square or polygonal towers when undermined. All the towers were connected by a curtain wall.

War damage (right)

The château stood for many hundreds of years and began to decay. The architect Eugène Viollet-le-Duc restored and renovated the château in the nineteenth century. However, it was almost completely destroyed in 1917, when the German army dynamited the keep and four towers in their retreat near the end of World War I.

BUILDING TALL

Lighthouse of Alexandria

location: *Alexandria, Egypt*

architect: *Ptolemy I Soter*

completed: *ca. 280 BCE*

Tall buildings do not provide only material or aesthetic power, they can also be useful instruments of peace and protection. Built by Ptolemy I Soter, the Lighthouse of Alexandria (or Pharos of Alexandria) alerted ships to the great harbor of the city. It was one of the Seven Wonders of the World, and survived into the twelfth century. Although its exact dimensions are lost, the lighthouse is thought to have reached 350 feet (107 m), and its remains are built into the Citadel of Qā'it Bāy and can be found in surrounding waters.

Ancient remains

A team of archaeologists in 1968, and another in 1995, rediscovered the remains of the lighthouse. Subsequently, satellite imaging has revealed further evidence, and there are rumors of plans for reconstruction of this ancient wonder. Although earthquake damage had rendered it a ruin by the fourteenth century, its depiction by artists and engravers down the ages gives an impression of its original magnificent architecture.

Three tiers (below)

The lighthouse was tiered in three sections, suggesting three separate construction stages: a wide square base, an octagonal shaft, and cylindrical top. A spiral ramp curled around to provide access. It was surmounted by a platform and fire.

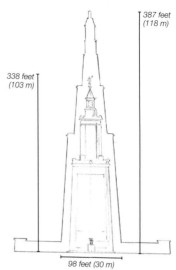

387 feet (118 m)

338 feet (103 m)

98 feet (30 m)

Disputed dimensions (above)

The exact height of the lighthouse remains unknown. Later Arabic observers provide a more consistent picture, with variations from 338 to 387 feet (103 to 118 m). The base has been consistently given as 98 feet (30 m) wide.

Island location

The lighthouse was built on the island of Pharos. A vast mole (the Heptastadion) was constructed between the island and the new city of Alexandria. The Heptastadion formed a harbor on the east side and a port on its west side.

Lighthouse of Pharos

Palace quarter

The great harbor

Jewish quarter

Isle of Pharos

The Heptastadion

ALEXANDRIA

Lake Mareotis

Jantar Mantar

location: *Jaipur, India*
completed: *1734*

Heritage site
The instrument is constructed of local stone faced in marble, with bronze and tile details. Although by the nineteenth century Jantar Mantar had fallen into disrepair, it has subsequently been restored and maintained. Accurate or not, these colossal instruments remain a wonder and are now a UNESCO World Heritage Site.

In the early eighteenth century, the northern Indian ruler of Rajput, Maharaja Sawai Jai Singh II, ordered the construction of 19 architectural astronomical instruments. These instruments were designed to improve the various prescientific astronomical systems of calculation known in the world at the time. As well as an array of instruments designed to locate and measure celestial bodies in the sky, a number of sundials were made, including the Vrihat Samrat Yantra ("supreme instrument")—the world's largest sundial, reaching 88 feet (27 m) in height. Jai Singh was also responsible for the construction of the city that bears his name—Jaipur—the design of which was based on the ancient Hindu grid pattern discovered in ruins that date back to the third century CE.

Giant clock (below)

Jai Singh assumed that the sheer scale of Samrat Yantra would provide a more accurate measure of time than made with traditional sundials. Each quadrant is marked with degrees, and the shadow from the gnomon can be seen passing at a rate of ³⁄₆₄ inch (1 mm) per second. But the desired increase in accuracy sought from building such enormous instruments has been questioned. The fluctuating penumbra of the sun, crafting of the instruments by stonemasons used to working with higher tolerances, and subsidence over time, all introduce inaccuracies.

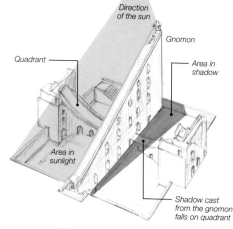

Direction of the sun

Gnomon

Quadrant

Area in shadow

Area in sunlight

Shadow cast from the gnomon falls on quadrant

Measuring time (above)

The Samrat Yantra differs little from typical sundials. The shadow cast from the centered "gnomon" (the large triangular wall) falls on quadrants on each side. The hypotenuse of the gnomon is parallel to the earth's axis, and the quadrants lie parallel to the equator.

Supreme instruments

The Samrat Yantra is but one of many astronomical instruments designed and constructed on a colossal scale. Although strictly a scientific failure, these giant works offer powerful reminders of the enduring relation between architecture and cosmic study and speculation.

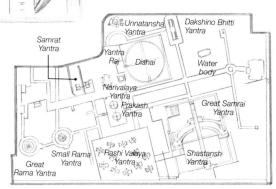

Samrat Yantra

Unnatansha Yantra

Dakshino Bhitti Yantra

Yantra Raj   Dishai

Water body

Narivalaya Yantra

Prakash Yantra

Great Samrai Yantra

Great Rama Yantra

Small Rama Yantra

Rashi Valaya Yantra

Shastansh Yantra

33

Introduction

The Big Apple
The city that become world-famous for its skyline, New York's skyscrapers of the early twentieth century were a product of its earlier development at the heart of industrial transatlantic trade.

The modern skyscraper is the product of a number of developments. Such tall buildings required fundamental technological advances. To be sure that height did not compromise safety, lightweight, strong structures were needed, which favored steel frames over load-bearing masonry walls. Tall building design must include the swift, secure, vertical transportation of people and materials, which required the invention of the elevator. The skyscraper's internal environments, the height and exposure of which produce extreme temperatures and humidity levels, also needed mechanical conditioning. However, having the technical ability to build tall is only part of the skyscraper story. Strong economic, political, and cultural forces played their part: the

urban plan of New York City and Chicago, the concentration of corporate wealth in commercial districts, and fierce competition between the two cities.

Finally, the physical forms of skyscrapers were determined as much by external factors, such as urban zoning, air-space regulation, and symbolism, as any commercial, practical, or architectural motive. In the nineteenth century, buildings were the most powerful and far-reaching means of communication. Yet even as their reach was surpassed by first newsprint, then photography, radio, and film, right up to the present day, in an age of cell phones and social media, the skyscraper remains an iconic form, signifying wealth, dominance, and dynamism in the urban landscape.

The Windy City
Chicago, rebuilt after fire devastated the city in 1871, is the historical birthplace of the skyscraper. Nicknamed the "Windy City" by rivalrous New Yorkers, Chicago competed with the East Coast metropolis for supremacy in both commerce and architecture.

Ditherington Flax Mill

location: *Shropshire, UK*
architect: *Charles Bage (structural engineer)*
completion: *ca. 1796/ 1800*

Restoration of the mill

The original mill was 174 feet (53 m) long and 36 feet (11 m) wide. Bage's innovative design ensured the building's structural integrity without the need for internal walls. The building operated as a flax mill until 1886 when it was converted to a maltings for the brewing industry. One century on, the maltings closed and the building became derelict until 2005, when work on its restoration began.

Between the Shropshire towns of Shrewsbury and Ditherington in England, within a bend of the Severn River, stands what may seem to be an unprepossessing brick building. Everything appears to be designed to hide the significance of perhaps the most important industrial heritage site in England. Built between 1796 and 1800, the original flax mill, designed by a local engineer, Charles Bage, was the first multistory iron-frame building in the world. Ditherington Flax Mill has been dubbed the "grandfather of the skyscraper," because its column-and-beam metalwork was the precursor to the steel-frame structure needed for the construction of the modern skyscraper.

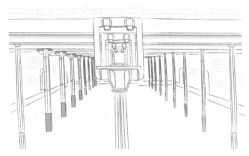

Iron frame (left)

The iron frame provides five stories and 18 bays. Between each bay, 16 two-piece, cast-iron transverse beams, joined at their centers, span the width of the building, supported by three rows of cast-iron columns forming a rigid frame.

Wrought-iron roof struts (right)

Each column is cruciform in cross section and molded at base and capital. Wrought-iron tie rods run axially between the beams, tying the iron frame together. The top floor is covered by inclined brick vaults that spring from the beams.

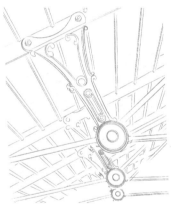

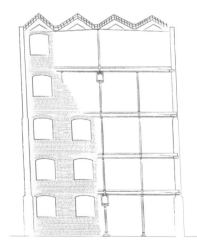

Section (left)

At 18 inches (46 cm) thick, the external walls of the building provide additional support to the frame within. Red "great" bricks were used—measuring $4 \times 9\frac{1}{2} \times 4\frac{1}{2}$ inches (10 x 24 x 11 cm)—with setbacks at each level, both external and internal. Although many are no longer visible, all openings in each bay were originally large.

Crystal Palace

NEW MATERIALS

location: *London, UK*
architect: *Joseph Paxton*
completion: *1851*

**Contemporary
perspective painting**
The Crystal Palace
was 1,851 feet (564 m)
long and 128 feet (39 m)
tall, large enough to
encompass mature trees
in the royal park and to
house not only products
from around the world
but the factory engines
used to produce them.

The Crystal Palace, first erected in 1851 in London's Hyde Park as the main pavilion for the Great Exhibition of that year, has been heralded as one of the great wonders of modern engineering and architecture. Designed by the landscape gardener and glass house designer Joseph Paxton, the Crystal Palace combined the most sophisticated building technologies and techniques of its day—iron-frame structure and glass covering, using standardized prefabricated parts manufactured in factories and delivered to the site by rail. The building was relocated to the south London suburbs in 1854, where it stood until it was destroyed by fire in 1936.

Building the Palace

Although massive in scale, Paxton's design and the production process meant that building could be quickly constructed. Lightweight, and composed of standardized parts using the same fitting process, it took only six months to complete.

Elevation (below)

Paxton's was a design of economy, costing one-third of any rival design submitted, and he designed it on a modular basis. The basic unit he used were the dimensions of the largest sheets of plate glass that could be manufactured by Chance Brothers, a company that became known as the greatest glass manufacturer in Great Britain.

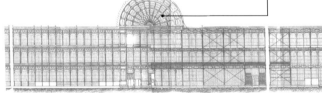

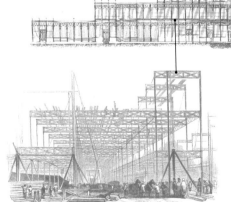

Cross section (left)

The Crystal Palace has a repeating section—the same structure is reproduced along the length of the building—and each section is self-supporting. This made the building limitless; the sections could be repeated infinitely in either direction without consequence.

Eiffel Tower

Tour de force
Gustave Eiffel, the
tower's designer, was
a highly successful
civil engineer, who
also contributed to the
structural design of New
York's Statue of Liberty.
For Eiffel, the design of
the Tower represented
Enlightenment values
and the spirit of the
French Revolution.

Arguably one of the most iconic structures of all, the
Eiffel Tower was completed in 1889 and marked the
entrance to the *Exposition Universelle* (world fair) that
year. At 1,063 feet (324 m; roughly equivalent to an
81-story building), it was the world's tallest building
for 41 years. There are few parts of Paris from which
the tower cannot be seen, and it remains the most
visited paid attraction in the world; an estimated more
than 300 million people had visited by the end of 2017.
Albeit not the first multistory building to rely entirely
on an iron frame (that was a humble warehouse in the
St.-Ouen docks), Eiffel's tower was the most remarkable.

location: *Paris, France*
architect: *Gustave Eiffel*
completion: *1889*

Going up (right)

There are more than 700 steps to the second platform. To support high visitor numbers, elevators were installed in two of the pillars, taking visitors in stages to the first and then second platforms. A further series of cars was installed for travel between the third and final platform.

Elevation (below)

The tower consists of four lattice girders, constituting four gigantic pillars. From four corners, these rise up toward the center and eventually join. The pillars are bound together by three trusses that form viewing platforms. The tower is further embellished with four nonstructural arches and other decorative ironwork.

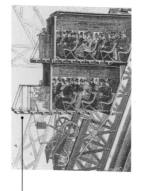

The early elevator cabins had pivoted floor sections, leveled by the operator to compensate for the change in inclination

Cross sections

The tower's four "legs" are anchored in limestone "shoes," set in reinforced concrete slabs. The legs form a 410-foot (125-m) square base. Rising to 186 feet (57 m), they are joined together by the first platform. The tower is capped with a viewing platform and radio mast.

Sixteen anchors lock each leg to the concrete slabs

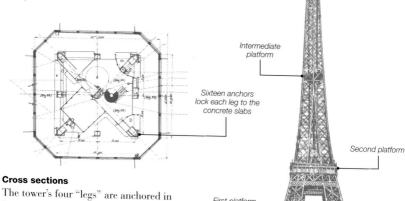

Third platform

Intermediate platform

Second platform

First platform

Invention of the Safety Elevator

location: *New York, USA*
inventor: *Elisha Otis*
completion: *1853*

At the Crystal Palace Exhibition Hall in New York, in 1853, crowds gathered to watch the mechanical hoisting of a man standing on a platform. A rope, suspended from the ceiling, heaved the platform and its cargo upward. Another man was invited to cut the rope with an ax, and to gasps in the crowd, the platform remained suspended in the air. The purpose of the demonstration was to show that Elisha Otis had invented the first viable safety elevator, a prerequisite to the occupancy of multistory buildings. The Otis Elevator Company is still trading today, with billion-dollar revenues.

Hold the elevator
The first commercial elevator installed by Otis was at a department store on Broadway and Broome Street, New York, in 1857. By then, developers of large commercial buildings in the city had already begun to specify vacant shafts, sure in their belief that elevators would be invented that could safely carry passengers.

Demonstrating the safety elevator

By convincing the public of the efficacy of his safety-locking feature, Otis paved the way for the global proliferation of the skyscrapers. His passenger elevators were soon to be installed in the Eiffel Tower, the Empire State Building, the Kremlin, and, in the twenty-first century, in the megatall Burj Khalifa, which has 65 Otis elevators.

Safety locking (right)

The early safety elevator locked into place if the rope was cut—"shoes" would press against the sides of the platform and, through friction, prevent it from falling. Elevators now have numerous safety mechanisms in place to prevent a drop—if the cable that hauls the elevator fails, it would have no effect, other than to stop the elevator from moving.

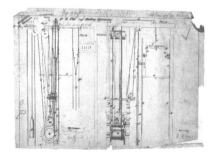

Adapting the safety elevator (left)

The Otis Elevator Company invented hydraulic, electric, steam, and belt elevators. More than 160 years after the safety elevator was patented, the Otis company continues to adapt—one recently developed system is solar power capable.

Development of Fireproofing Systems

Theatre Royal Drury Lane, London, UK
The candles used in many theaters presented a significant fire threat. London's Drury Lane theater twice burned down before being rebuilt in 1812. That same building still stands today.

The development of the skyscraper is intimately related to the risk of fire. The disastrous Great Chicago Fire of 1871, and the subsequent rebuilding of the city, resulted in the advancement of skyscrapers, and the need to protect (and insure) against fire drove engineers to develop fire-suppressing systems, especially the automatic sprinkler.

Theater interior (right)

An early form of sprinkler system was designed and installed at London's Drury Lane, in England, in 1812. The architect, William Congreve, conceived of a system fed by a large reservoir of water contained in a cylinder under pressure. This could be released into an overhead branching system of pipes with small holes that could dampen a fire.

Nature's sprinkler (left)

The Great Chicago Fire of 1871 was finally brought under control on October 10, when rain assisted firefighting efforts. Reconstruction began immediately, laying the foundations for the world's first skyscrapers. It was not until 2004 that Chicago City Council made it mandatory for all commercial buildings to be retrofitted with fire sprinkler systems.

Early automatic sprinkler

Until the late nineteenth century, sprinkler systems were manual—someone needed to release water into the system. A succession of inventions and patents from the 1860s onward eventually crystallized in Frederick Grinnell's designs. His modification of an early automatic system by Henry S. Parmalee resulted in the design of a glass disk device in 1890, one that we still recognize today.

Glass valve

Main strut piece

Hook on strut

Deflector plate

Ventilation

Art Deco design

Even the humble door was transformed by the advent of the skyscraper. Groups of tall buildings act like canyons, sucking through air at high speeds. A revolving door prevents drafts from forcing the entrance open or slamming it shut. Revolving doors have since become a beautiful feature in their own right: those on the Marine Building in Vancouver, Canada, are a glorious example of Art Deco architecture.

Skyscrapers embody a succession of technological innovations. The steel frame made it practicable to build tall. The elevator made that building habitable by large numbers of people. The sprinkler system prevents those occupants from being exposed to fire risk. But, once buildings of skyscraper height are constructed—particularly ones enveloped in thin, lightweight, transparent materials, such as glass—new environmental challenges arise. Glass lets a lot of heat in and out, requiring temperatures to be regulated to make conditions within comfortable. And as heat is lost from the surface of a skyscraper, warm air is drawn up from the lower levels, resulting in great updrafts, overheating, and rapid cooling of air.

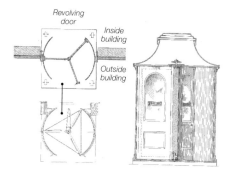

Early revolving doors

Simple mechanical solutions are available to solve the problem of inward-rushing air. Revolving doors—utilized in buildings with large traffic for some time—came into their own at the end of the nineteenth century, and were perfected to "filter" the ground openings—allowing for the simultaneous entry and exit of people, but keeping wind out.

Early boiler and vent system

Domestic "central heating" systems, particularly through hot water radiators, had been developed in the nineteenth century. However, buildings the size of skyscrapers required low-pressure steam and fan-driven air systems to heat.

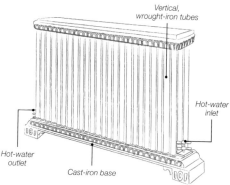

Early air-conditioning

Mechanical ventilation and cooling of air had also been advanced by the 1870s. Early skyscraper architects struggled to find room for the enormous quantities of plant and ducting required for mechanical ventilation, resolved only at the beginning of the twentieth century with the development of electrical air-conditioning units.

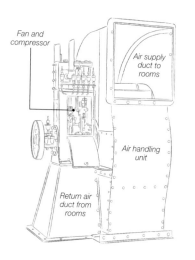

Electricity

Early skyscrapers had to be lit using gas-lighting systems. The vulnerability of steel-frame buildings to fire—and the exposure to risk of so many people within them—made this solution to lighting a real danger. Once electrical lighting had proved viable, skyscrapers were the first type of building to take up the new technology with gusto. And lighting was only one use for electrical power in tall buildings. Air-conditioning, water pumps, heating—all could be powered by electricity. Soon apartments and offices were equipped with a panoply of electrical appliances.

The city that never sleeps

First with the incandescent bulb and then with fluorescent lighting (which produced brighter light with little heat), skyscrapers created constant light within and spectacular landscapes without. New York City was able to work and play throughout the night, due to electrification.

Incandescent lamps

Thomas Edison was not the first to invent an incandescent lightbulb, but using a "carbon filament or strip coiled and connected" to contact wires, his patent of 1879 marked the commercialization of the idea. In 1880, the Edison Electric Light Company began marketing its product to the world.

Edison's electric power station

Edison not only developed a successful product that could consume electricity, he provided a source of electricity, too. His company built a power plant in the heart of downtown Manhattan, the Pearl Street Station, establishing a "grid" of cables that could power lightbulbs in a half-mile radius. Delivering low-voltage direct current, Edison attracted financial backers, including J. P. Morgan, like moths to a flame.

Welding the Empire State Building

Electricity was not only needed to modify the completed environment of the skyscraper—by the 1930s, it was being used to build the skyscraper. Arc welding, which was initially developed during World War I by the Americans and the British for building ships, rapidly advanced in the 1930s and was used to weld the framework of the Empire State Building, one quarter-mile above street level.

Railroads & Commerce

The Chicago "Loop"
Commercial and trading enterprises vied for space in central Chicago where the railroads met, causing congestion and land price pressures. This had two results: an elevated track (of 1897) to carry passengers from the major intercity lines and skyscraper development. The "Loop"—downtown Chicago—was born.

Much of the technology utilized in early skyscrapers— iron and steel frames, steam power, modular construction—was first developed in the railroad industries. However, the railroads provided more than simply technology. With the tendency to reinforce geographic centralization in major trading centers, such as New York City and Chicago, and with the concentration of capital within strong monopolies, railroad development set the stage for the skyscrapers of the late nineteenth century.

Cattle pens

Chicago became the meatpacker and grain silo of America. Slaughterhouses on an industrial scale meant new technologies: warehousing, refrigeration, and conveyor-belt production. These inventions and methods passed into other trades, including architecture, and simultaneously, the concentration and coordination of commerce in cities increased the demand for office space.

Commercial links

The railroads didn't only bring livestock to Chicago— they brought steel workers, engineers, surveyors, and financiers. From the slaughterhouses and meatpackers came the knowledge of how to build.

Chicago's railroad network

Chicago is the great hub of North American railroad traffic. Early lines were chartered for nonpassenger purposes in the 1830s— transporting minerals and wheat from mines and farms in the Midwest. By the 1870s, Chicago was connected by rail to every major city in the United States. It had also become a manufacturing center for locomotives and freight and passenger cars.

Grid Cities

New York grid

The city's grid system, originally laid out by the 1811 Commission, has been altered several times (most significantly in the 1850s with the introduction of Central Park). Avenues run from northeast to southwest and streets from southeast to northwest. These are cut diagonally by Broadway, which trickles from north to south.

The organization of urban areas in grids has been recognized since antiquity—both the ancient Romans and Chinese independently evolved approaches to urban planning based on grid forms. However, it is in the urban grids of the United States, set out in the eighteenth and nineteenth centuries, that the ground for the skyscraper was set out. In granting rights and privileges to landowners on discrete plots, the city block produced by grid planning allowed for speculative development and a new kind of investment.

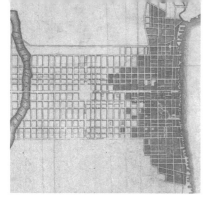

Plan of Philadelphia (left)

Inspired by aborted plans for the rebuilding of London following the Great Fire of 1666, the Quaker William Penn, founder of Pennsylvania State, proposed a grid city from which new settlers (and investors) could purchase plots of land. Penn's vision was of a pastoral idyll. The American city of the future would not turn out quite that way.

Commissioners' Plan, Manhattan (right)

Perhaps the most famous "grid" in the world, the planning of Manhattan was made at the beginning of the nineteenth century and finally realized in the publication of the Commissioners' Plan of 1811. Utilizing a rectangular grid, the plan allowed for rapid speculative development across the island, with minimal interference but maximal facilitation by public institutions.

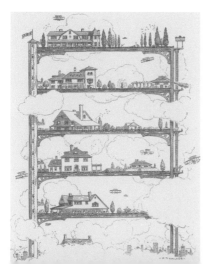

"Buy a cozy cottage . . ."

In a now infamous cartoon of 1909, the artist A. B. Walker satirized the condition of speculative development in Manhattan. In doing so, he also aptly summarized the way in which the skyscraper made the horizontal grid of real estate speculation vertical.

Zoning & Fire Regulation

Great Fire of Chicago
The 1871 fire destroyed Chicago's commercial heart but the railroads, stockyards, and docks were untouched. New regulations imposing expensive material controls to prevent fires transformed the city: ordinary residents could not afford to rebuild, but Chicago wealthy investors could build huge edifices of steel, stone, and terra-cotta.

The mass and shape of early skyscrapers was produced by more than technological advance, or real estate speculation. One of the major spurs for the development of the skyscraper—the steel frame—was a product of fire regulation in the aftermath of the Great Fire of Chicago (1871). While the skyscraper posed unique problems for internal environmental controls, they also proved to have significant effects on the wider urban landscapes. Public regulation of building—controlling height, zoning, and regulating building materials—had major consequences for the emergence of the modern skyscraper.

Zoning laws (right)

The 1916 Zoning Ordinance of New York sought to restrict height, massing, and use for buildings in specific parts of the city. The illustrator and architect Hugh Ferris subsequently published, in 1922, a series of remarkable drawings, demonstrating the consequences of these zoning regulations for future skyscraper designs.

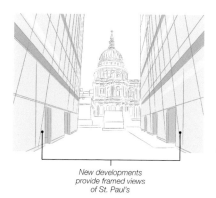

New developments provide framed views of St. Paul's

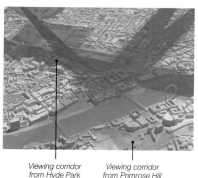

Viewing corridor from Hyde Park

Viewing corridor from Primrose Hill

Protected views (left and above left)

Other forms of regulation can have major consequences for the siting and design of skyscrapers. In London, UK, for example, views of St. Paul's Cathedral from specified points across the city, are protected in law. Known as "visual corridors," these determine whether tall buildings will be given permission and if so, what form they might take.

Media & Advertising

Newspaper Row
One of the earliest areas of Manhattan for concentrated high-rise development occurred near the City Hall. Newspapers were eager to be located as close as possible to the political heart of the city. Here, in what became known as "Newspaper Row," the *New York Tribune*, *New York Times*, and *New York World* competed for dominance.

The modern skyscraper was born of commercial and speculative real estate development. But it was also born of a need to communicate; even today, in the age of information technology, buildings have a spectacular power to reach millions. Simple, but often awe-inspiring, skyscrapers communicate a message of power and energy unlike any other building form. It is perhaps no surprise, then, that in the golden age of skyscraper building in the United States, major sponsors included those who knew all about sending out messages—the newspaper barons.

Movie moments (right)

Newspaper barons built the skyscrapers and, later, the movie industry promoted them. Hollywood came to dominate the movie market globally and created instant icons. Most successfully of all, King Kong, astride the Empire State Building, instantaneously fixed that building as a monument to modernity.

Taj Mahal, Atlantic City (below)

Today skyscrapers continue to be used as a means to promote corporate branding and even individuals. No longer confined to a domestic market, images of tall buildings circulate the globe, providing the real estate owner with highly valuable visibility.

Windy City (above)

Rivalry between Chicagoan and New Yorker newspaper barons and their sponsorship of local political elites reached a hot point in 1889 over the hosting of a "World Fair" celebrating the fourth centenary of Columbus's discovery of North America. New Yorkers dubbed Chicago the "Windy City," not because of its many skyscrapers (although they did channel winds from the Great Lakes), but for its people's arrogance.

Introduction

Lofty ambitions

A close circle of Chicago's architects combined utilitarian structural designs with the rapid advances in technology in their early skyscrapers. Trained at or influenced by the École des Beaux-Arts in Paris, they were also inspired by classical architecture of the Renaissance and antiquity, elements of which they used to embellish their designs.

The modern skyscraper as we know it was first produced in the great commercial cities of North America. From Chicago, rebuilding after the Great Fire of 1871, and with the resources, technology, and drive to build tall, came the skyscrapers of the "Commercial School," harbinger of "Functionalism" and the modern "International Style." Not to be outdone by its rival, ambitious projects in New York City began to dominate the skyline. From the 1880s to the 1940s, the United States experienced a transformation in its architectural aspirations, and the skyscraper passed through a number of stylistic changes.

Classical aesthetics dominated the early skyscrapers of New York until the 1910s, when its architects departed from the Chicago model. First, they introduced neo-Gothic treatments, styling their skyscrapers in the manner of medieval cathedrals. Then, in the 1920s, Art Nouveau and Art Deco styles emerged using stylized organic ornaments, based on the motifs of ancient Egypt, machined in steel, glass, brass, and neon lights. From the 1930s, skyscraper architects in both New York and Chicago eradicated ornamentation altogether in favor of a sleek, undecorated celebration of the advancement of building technology.

Home Insurance Building

location: *Chicago, USA*

architect: *William LeBaron Jenney / George B. Whitney (engineer)*

completed: *1885*

Work on the first true modern skyscraper began in Chicago in 1884. Designed by William LeBaron Jenney, the Home Insurance Building was the culmination of years of development in construction methods. Perhaps influenced by the "balloon-frame" timber construction of housing across the East Coast and Midwest, Jenney developed a "honeycomb" frame of cast- and wrought-iron columns and beams, and included some steel in the upper stories (the first time steel was used in a building in America). Other buildings, built soon after 1885, have been identified as using skeleton iron-frame designs, and some doubted whether Jenney's building used iron consistently. However, demolition of the Home Insurance Building in 1931 showed its reliance on an iron frame throughout.

Iron honeycomb

What made the Home Insurance Building the "first" skyscraper was its construction not height. At 138 feet (42 m) and with 10 stories (rising to 12 by 1890), the building was comparatively modest. But by developing the iron frame, Jenney found a solution to construction that was economical both in terms of materials and in providing much greater floor area. His solution became a model for the giants that soon followed.

Decorative dressing (right)

Jenney's design of the exterior of the building is strikingly different in character from the structural solution. He dressed the building in masonry and brick, and he used heavy decorative motifs to disguise the light, grid structure that actually supported the weight of the building.

Skeleton frame (left)

The Home Insurance Building was the first to use a "skeleton" iron frame, making it considerably lighter than stone, as well as fire-resistant—a key factor following the Great Fire of 1871. Wrought- and cast-iron columns and beams were bolted together with the masonry applied as a covering.

Classical proportions (right)

Jenney had trained in the École Centrale, Paris, and in designing the dressing of the building he adopted a "classical" approach. The base was set with heavy masonry, and highly decorated. His addition of a "lintel" to the top of the building made it appear closed and complete, and the street facades were symmetrical.

The Rookery

location: *Chicago, USA*

architects: *Burnham & Root*

completed: *1888*

The oldest standing high-rise building in the Chicago downtown area, the Rookery was designed by the partnership of Daniel Burnham and John Wellborn Root. Formerly the site of the Chicago City Hall (nicknamed the Rookery for the birds that would gather outside it, as well as the politicians who gathered within), 209 South LaSalle Street is a standout example of transitional architecture for commercial skyscrapers—unlike the Home Insurance Building (see page 60), the Rookery has load-bearing masonry walls and a steel-frame interior.

Floating foundation

One of the engineering innovations of the building cannot be seen: the floating slab base of reinforced concrete. Recognizing the problems of Chicago's soft subsoils, Burnham and Root carried their building on this raft. Later, even heavier buildings would have to develop further means to support their weight.

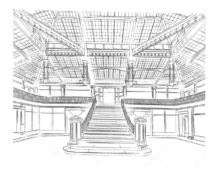

Light court

The most spectacular aspect of the Rookery is its galleried interior lobby. Burnham and Root included a deep glass atrium on the second floor. Between 1905 and 1907, Frank Lloyd Wright was commissioned to redesign the lobby interior. He replaced Root's iron railings and terra-cotta panels, introducing light fittings and pale marble. The result is an elegant iron-frame interior that maximizes light to all offices throughout the building.

Romanesque arch

Supporting the weight of such a tall building required heavy masonry at the base. The weight of this exterior masonry was visually reinforced by the use of a grand arch at the main entrance. Decorated by Burnham and Root in a Romanesque style reminiscent of the great American architect Henry Hobson Richardson, the arch belies the Modernism of the iron-frame building within.

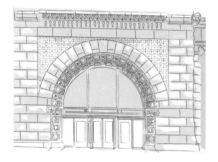

Oriel staircase

The beauty and elegance of the interior derives from the fine decorative treatment of the wrought-iron frame. This includes the heavily ornamented spiral staircases. Principal of these is the oriel staircase, designed by John Root, which descends ten floors into the lobby, increasing natural light and ventilation to the lower levels.

Monadnock Building

location: *Chicago, USA*
architects: *Burnham & Root / Holabird & Roche*
completed: *1893*

Standing on 53 West Jackson Boulevard is the startling Monadnock—named for the New England mountain. It is, in fact, a building of two halves—the North block, begun in 1881, and designed by Daniel Burnham and John Root, and the South, begun in 1891, and designed by William Holabird and Martin Roche, who had trained together under William LeBaron Jenney (see page 60). Each half in turn was designed as two sections, the four sections being (north to south), the Monadnock, the Kearsarge, the Katahdin, and the Wachusett. The building is impressive in height—the South block is 17 stories and 215 feet (66 m)—but it is famous for two reasons: the treatment of decoration on the North block by Burnham and Root; and the introduction of the skeleton frame by Holabird and Roche on the South block.

Windproof building

Although a masonry load-bearing construction, the Monadnock did introduce technical developments to the skyscraper. As well as an interior iron frame, Root devised an early version of an iron portal frame, as a form of wind brace. Iron struts were riveted between the columns, adding strength to the frame.

The North block (1881–91)

Burnham and Root needed to build on a narrow site, using load-bearing walls. As a result, the walls at the ground level are 6 feet (1.8 m) thick—thicker still below ground. The facade of the North block was devoid of any ornamentation, a businesslike aesthetic that set the standard for the American commercial skyscraper.

The South block (1891–93)

The South phase was designed so that the walls were "hung" from the interior frame. No piers or thick granite were required, and the lower floors had as much space and light as the upper. Holabird and Roche still designed the "ground" differently from the rest of the building, but for functional and aesthetic, not constructional reasons.

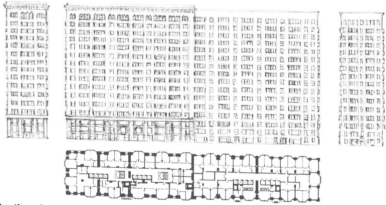

Another view

The Monadnock provides a great example of the development of the Chicago "Commercial School"—the North block still has one foot in the architecture of the past but strips away ornamentation and gains aesthetic power from an unadorned grid of openings. The South block embraces the full potential of Jenney's iron-and-steel frame, freeing space in the interior and on the facade of the building.

The Reliance Building

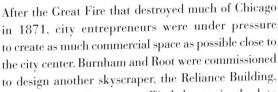

location: *Chicago, USA*

architects: *Burnham & Root / D. H. Burnham & Co. / Charles Atwood*

completed: *1895*

After the Great Fire that destroyed much of Chicago in 1871, city entrepreneurs were under pressure to create as much commercial space as possible close to the city center. Burnham and Root were commissioned to design another skyscraper, the Reliance Building, in the Loop area. Work began in the late 1880s, but Root died in 1891 with only the foundations and base of the 14-story building complete. Burnham continued with designer Charles Atwood and engineer Edward Shankland. Shankland introduced radical new approaches to steel-frame engineering and Atwood pushed the limits of architectural design and expression to produce a style that many historians have understood as a precursor to later twentieth-century Modernism. Together, they would come to redefine the Chicago "Commercial School" of architecture.

Clean exterior

On completion, the building was leased to merchant traders and medical professionals. Its architects sought to maximize the natural light, particularly for the offices used by medics, and Ashwood specified large windows and glazed terra-cotta tiles to create a surface that exuded clinical hygiene. Its shining white facade remains the building's most distinguishing feature.

Open-frame structure

Shankland engineered the Reliance Building through two major areas of innovation—adding 25-foot-deep piles (about 7.6 m) to the reinforced concrete float (allowing for it to withstand even greater pressures) and designing the steel frame so that all cross bracing (for wind resistance) was removed. This produced an open frame that Atwood could cover with glass and tile.

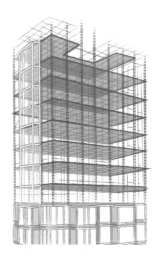

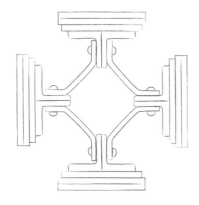

The Gray column (left)

That Shankland could produce such an engineered solution was due to his use of the "Gray column." This type of steel column—hollow, simple to manufacture, and providing enough flat plate surface for riveting—could withstand bending moments from any direction, and, therefore, could withstand wind.

Terra-cotta and glass

Atwood's design was controversial but proved highly influential. The justification for large quantities of glass and terra-cotta was practical (or "functional"): the glass allowed for more light, and the white glazed terra-cotta was supposed to be self-cleaning. But it was the aesthetic effect that proved so powerful for the first time—the skyscraper appeared as a steel frame, hung with glass.

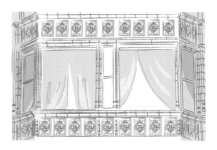

18 South Michigan Avenue

location: *Chicago, USA*
architects: *Holabird & Roche / Louis Sullivan*
completed: *1899*

Number 18 South Michigan Avenue is the last in a row of three buildings built at the same time (1890–99). At first sight, these read as completely different buildings—different in height, width, ornament, and color. But they were all part of a group (the Gage Group Buildings), designed by Holabird & Roche, for three millinery firms: Gage, Keith, and Ascher. As skyscrapers, numbers 18, 24, and 30 share some basic design principles. Number 18, the tallest, stands out with its exceptional decorative treatment. It was completed by Louis Sullivan, and is one of only five buildings in Chicago designed by him that survive.

The Gage Group Buildings

Today, numbers 30 and 24, designed by Holabird & Roche, look much as they did originally, but a further level was added to number 30 in 1971. Functional in design, the facades emphasize the underlying steel-frame structure. Although the buildings are not the same width, both have exactly the same glazing and tile proportions. Number 18, however, is different. Originally only one story higher than number 24, it completely broke with the group when four stories were added in 1902 by different architects.

Exterior ornament (left and above)

Sullivan and his architect George G. Elmslie applied ornamentation to their building at number 18, which created two strong visual effects. The application of two "columns" or "piers," with fluting and a highly ornate floral burst at the caps, emphasizes the height of the building. The patterning of the tiles, which are set almost flush with the glazed windows and are deeply recessed (compared with the applied columns), suggests a very thin hanging face, almost like a textile.

Commercial architecture

As with so many Chicago School buildings of the late nineteenth century, 18 South Michigan Avenue was not treated kindly in the mid-twentieth century. Dismissed as just "commercial" architecture, unworthy of conservation, the delicate facade was hidden for much of the mid-century decades behind fire escapes, commercial hoardings, and storefronts.

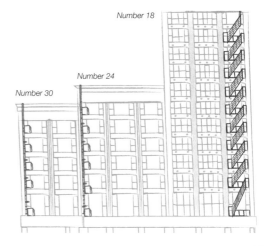

Number 18

Number 24

Number 30

Schiller Building

location: *Chicago, USA*

architects: *Dankmar Adler and Louis Sullivan*

completed: *1891*

One of the great collaborative works of Louis Sullivan and Dankmar Adler, the Schiller Building, or Garrick Theater, Chicago, was built at 64 West Randolph Street for the German Opera Company. Adler's engineering ensured an elegant solution to the problem of a tall building (240 feet/73 m) that contained a large auditorium. Sullivan provided sophisticated ornamentation that accentuated the height of the building and celebrated the cavernous vaults of the theatrical auditorium. Falling into disuse and disrepair, despite a battle to save it, the building was demolished and replaced with a parking lot in 1961. The destruction caused outrage, encouraging a movement to conserve modern buildings in the United States.

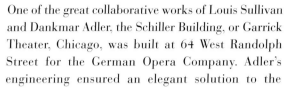

"A proud and soaring thing"

From the street, the 14-floor Schiller Building was one of the tallest buildings in Chicago. Sullivan decorated the facade so that it appeared at the base as a gently curved arcade. Above this rose a tall main tower, winged by two shorter towers, half its height. By using a setback, Sullivan could provide greater light to all offices and rooms throughout the building.

Longitudinal section (left)

Adler incorporated a number of engineering innovations, one of which was the piled concrete rafts—including eight hundred 50-foot (15-m) wooden piles, driven into the soft Chicago clay subsoil. In approach, the rafts prefigured later caisson design. Adler also used 93-foot-high (28 m) "Phoenix columns" (manufactured by the eponymous company of Pennsylvania) to support the building above the auditorium.

Auditorium (right)

Characteristic of Sullivan's work, the vaults of the 1,286-seat auditorium were highly decorated. The deep ridges of the vault were faced with plaster panels, molded with distinct abstract stellar shapes, and bordered with organic vine-and-leaf-patterns. Designed by Sullivan's office, some elements of pattern have been attributed to the young Frank Lloyd Wright.

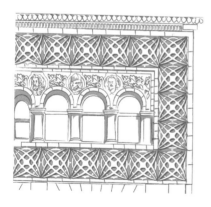

Exterior decoration

The exterior was as lavishly decorated as the interior. The upper "cornice" of the tower was faced with terra-cotta tiles, molded in a highly refined arabesque motif, punctuated by busts of German poets, musicians, and actors. These luminaries were also visible above the theater's arched entrance. Sullivan saw the decoration as an important means of expressing the organization of the building—its base, intermediary, and cap articulated in the applied ornamentation.

Chicago Stock Exchange

location: *Chicago, USA*

architects: *Dankmar Adler and Louis Sullivan*

completed: *1893*

Standing alone, outside the Art Institute of Chicago, is a monumental but delicately ornamented arch. It is all that remains of the original Chicago Stock Exchange, designed by Adler and Sullivan in 1893. Thirteen stories high, the Stock Exchange Building exemplified Adler and Sullivan's approach to skyscraper design, integrating a classical sense of ornamentation with modern technology. However, in the Stock Exchange Building, Sullivan reduced his ornamental flamboyance, and Adler resolved his technological fix of building subsidence common in the city.

Exterior

The exterior of the Stock Exchange Building marked a transitional moment in skyscraper design and its regulation in the city of Chicago. In 1893, a new fire code restricted the depth and increased the required spacing between bay windows. Sullivan and Adler reacted with shallower, narrower oriels across the facade.

Stock Exchange arch

The remaining arch from the original Stock Exchange is made of terra-cotta, embellished with Sullivan's trademark arabesque ornamentation. In the spandrels of the arch are two large medallions, one depicting the house of Philip Peck (who was a founding figure of Chicago's history and from a wealthy and influential family), which formerly stood on the Stock Exchange site, and the other emblazoned with 1893, the date of the building's completion.

Trading floor (right)

When the Stock Exchange Building faced demolition in 1972, fragments of its spectacular trading floor were salvaged and incorporated into the Art Institute of Chicago in 1977. Architects Vinci and Kenny created a complete reconstruction of the room, faithfully reproducing the Romanesque columns and Sullivan's arabesque plasterwork, glasswork, and stencils.

Longitudinal section looking north

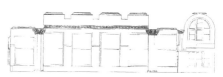

Longitudinal section looking west

Caisson foundations

Adler first deployed caisson foundations at the Stock Exchange Building. Most of the building is supported by wooden piles, similar to other skyscrapers by Sullivan and Adler. To prevent any damage to neighboring buildings, borrowing a technique used in bridge construction, Adler deployed a caisson on the west side—boring a hole and filling it with reinforced concrete.

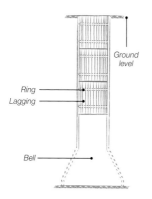

Ground level

Ring

Lagging

Bell

The Flatiron

At the turn of the twentieth century, New Yorkers witnessed the completion of the first skyscraper to rival Chicago: the Flatiron, designed by Chicago's great architect Daniel H. Burnham. It rose 22 stories, 285 feet (87 m) in the air, and was the city's tallest building north of 14th Street. Burnham brought the classical and commercial design ethos of Chicago, an approach that New York architects would soon emulate and quickly surpass. Its slender profile on a corner plot ensured the offices within were filled with light and air but, viewed from the street, it remains one of the most recognizable skyscrapers in New York and the world.

location: *New York, USA*
architect: *Daniel Burnham*
completed: *1902*

Slimline icon

The triangular form of the Flatiron is a product of its plot. The building sits, wedged between 5th Avenue and Broadway, opposite the west corner of Madison Square Park. The resulting plan is like a "flatiron," (or steam iron). The building was to be named the Fuller Building, after the major general contractor of the day, the Fuller Company, which specialized in skyscraper construction. However, the name "flatiron" stuck.

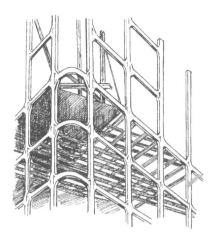

Rapid construction

The construction process was one of the more efficient in the period. Steel skeleton design was made possible in New York City with the redrafting of fire safety regulations in 1892, eliminating the need for masonry. With prefabricated steel components delivered efficiently, the structure of the Flatiron was assembled at a rate of one floor a week.

Classical order

Burnham relied on the classical ordering of the facade that he had used in many of his designs in Chicago. This meant that the building as a whole was treated as a Renaissance palazzo—a tripartite division between base, main body, and cap. The top of the Flatiron has heavy cornicing, and just below it, adding even greater emphasis, two massive Corinthian columns and various medallions and heads.

Retail space

Solid base

Burnham sought to retain the classical balance between the heavy cornice above and the base below. The center of the east face (on Broadway) indicates how he tried to achieve this, with much larger openings and hefty columns. These are matched with a pair of Corinthian columns at the tip of the north corner—but the client, Harry S. Black, insisted that it be extended and used as retail space.

Singer Building

In 1905, Frederick Bourne, head of the Singer Sewing Machine Co., commissioned the architect Ernest Flagg to design an extension to the company's headquarters on Broadway and Liberty Street in downtown Manhattan. Flagg produced a design for what became, briefly (1908–9), the tallest building in the world. Flagg approached his task as a Beaux-Arts architect—classically trained and with the firm belief that a building should be finely decorated. In the end, the Singer Building is as famous for its demise in 1968—it remains the tallest building in the world to be deliberately demolished by its owner.

location: *New York, USA*
architect: *Ernest Flagg*
completed: *1908*

Setback

In contrast to the dominant approach to building skyscrapers in New York at the time, Flagg firmly adhered to the principle that buildings more than 15 stories tall should be set back from the street. From street level, the Singer Building fills the block front, up to 14 stories. The remainder of the total 41 stories is achieved with a tower, so narrow that its footprint is only 65 square feet (6 m²).

Interior of the lobby

The lobby of the Singer Building was spectacularly decorated. Its floors and walls were marble, and glazed pendentive domes were supported by marble columns. Atop each column were bronze medallions, which were etched with the initials of the Singer Company, formed from a needle and thread motif.

Singer Building at night

The Singer Building was designed to stand out—and it was one of the first skyscrapers to be lit at night. Using huge arc lamps, the distinctive tower of the building could be seen across Manhattan, marking the skyline and advertising the sewing machine company to the world. This would set a trend for future skyscrapers.

Facade entrance

Throughout the Singer Building the service spaces were decorated with iron work and bronze—nowhere more so than the main east entrance to the building. Some 24 feet (7.3 m) high and 13 feet (4 m) wide, 4 tons of delicate bronze bars and scrolls suspended an ornate clockface.

Woolworth Building

location: *New York, USA*
architect: *Cass Gilbert*
completed: *1913*

"Cathedral of commerce"

Gilbert designed the building as a "setback" skyscraper—much like the Singer Building (see page 76)—maximizing the footprint at the ground but receding to become a single tower. Inspired by Gothic cathedrals, he incorporated massive piers that soar uninterrupted from ground to crown, reinforcing the vertical impact, and he applied limestone-colored panels to the facade (restoration in the twentieth century replaced the panels with concrete.)

Throughout 1910, the retail entrepreneur Frank Winfield Woolworth, founder of the first successful five-and-dime stores in the United States, purchased a large amount of property on Broadway. He commissioned the architect Cass Gilbert to design a 20-story headquarters for his growing retail empire. Gilbert eventually designed a 792-foot (241-m), 60-story giant of a skyscraper that continues to dominate the city skyline. Combining advanced technology with medieval styling, the Woolworth Building epitomizes early New York skyscraper design. On completion in 1913, the Woolworth Building was the tallest in the world and retained its title until 1930. It remains in the top 100 tallest buildings in the country.

Copper crown

The "crown" of the Woolworth building is treated with ornate, Gothic-inspired applied decoration. This decoration is oversized— huge pinnacles, lancet windows, gargoyles, and gigantic copper panels on the pyramidal spire are scaled up so that they can be read from street level some 700 feet (213 m) below.

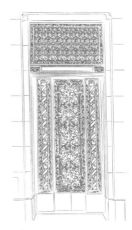

Elevator elegance

The Woolworth Building wasn't only well dressed. Engineers Gunvald Aus and Kort Berle designed its steel frame and installed the fastest elevators of the day, encased in tapering shafts that produced air cushioning were they to fall. This technology allowed for the Woolworth Building to provide maximum office to elevator ratios, securing high profitability for its owner.

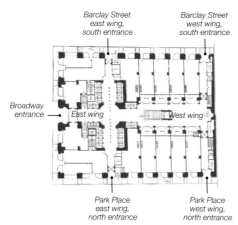

Barclay Street east wing, south entrance

Barclay Street west wing, south entrance

Broadway entrance

East wing

West wing

Park Place east wing, north entrance

Park Place west wing, north entrance

Cruciform lobby plan

The lobby of the Woolworth Building follows the neo-Gothic approach and is organized in cruciform. The space is dominated by Romanesque arches that are further ornamented in neo-Gothic embellishments. Richly marbled, with mosaic floor and ceiling, the lobby and the exterior inspired the Woolworth Building's moniker "cathedral of commerce."

Equitable Building (Manhattan)

location: *New York, USA*
architect: *Peirce Anderson*
completed: *1915*

The headquarters for the Equitable Life Insurance Co. was designed by Ernest R. Graham & Associates (the successor partnership to Daniel H. Burnham & Co.) and Peirce Anderson was its lead architect. At 538 feet (164 m), it wasn't the tallest building in the world, or even in New York. It did not particularly advance the structural technology of the day. But it influenced skyscraper design for decades to come, because in terms of floor area, it was the biggest office building in the world. Rising directly from the street, the design achieved the highest ratio of usable office space to land through uncompromising classical principles: no setbacks and no tower—resulting in a solid mass of building.

Exterior of Equitable

Although only 40 stories, the Equitable Building registers 1.2 million square feet (111,500 m²) of floor space on a plot smaller than an acre (4,050 m²). Relentlessly symmetrical and axially organized, the Equitable Building was a complete rejection of the neo-Gothic, setback design applied to the Woolworth Building (see page 78) and other skyscrapers of its time.

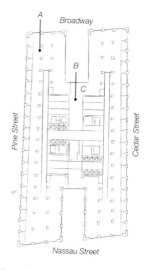

Broadway

Pine Street

Cedar Street

Nassau Street

H plan of the building

The organization of the building is an H plan: two enormous wings (A) are joined by a continuous centered bridging block (B). At the base is a through block lobby, marked with a gigantic barrel vault entrance on Broadway (C). Symmetrically planned throughout, the building attempts a rigorous classical approach to design.

Vaulted entrance

The entrance through the centered barrel vault demonstrates the relentlessly symmetrical and axially organized design of the building and Graham's complete rejection of the neo-Gothic.

Shadow cast

The distinctive design became influential for all the wrong reasons. Casting a 7-acre (28,300 m²) shadow on the surrounding streets, and a permanent shadow up to the 27th floor of the Singer Building (see page 76) and over all smaller buildings, the Equitable Building caused outrage. Fearing the loss of sunlight at street level to canyons of skyscraper, the 1916 Zoning Resolution was enacted, requiring setbacks and imposing height restrictions.

American Radiator Building

location: *New York, USA*
architects: *John Howells and Raymond Hood*
completed: *1924*

At only 23 stories, 338 feet (103 m), the American Radiator Building was never the tallest building in the world or even in New York City. But it set the standard for skyscraper design during the 1920s and 30s. Designed by John Howells and Raymond Hood in 1924, and decorated by the sculptor Rene Paul Chambellan, the American Radiator Building marked the transition from neo-Gothic to Art Deco architectural design and heralded a new wave of iconic skyscrapers.

Radiating style
Raymond Hood had just won the biggest skyscraper competition of the day—the Chicago Tribune Building. But a losing entry—by Eliel Saarinen—for a freestanding tower inspired Hood's design for the American Radiator. Instead of using the footprint of the plot, Hood set the tower back, allowing for light to flood in—and out—of the building.

Exuding heat and light

Hood and Howells faced their tower with black brick. The color was intended to represent coal—the main fuel for power in the United States at that time—solid and enduring. This choice also meant that the windows appeared not as "holes" in the facade but as bright lights against the dark silhouette. The building was trimmed with gold-color bricks (to symbolize fire), picking out the detailing.

Decorative panels

Chambellan was commissioned to provide sculptural relief work on the exterior and interior. These panels displayed allegorical images of material transformation or transmutation—symbolizing the transfer of mechanical heat (the main product of the American Radiator company). Chambellan's stylized antique sculpture inspired a generation of Art Deco design.

Chiaroscuro lighting

Hood disliked obtrusive street and arc lighting of skyscrapers. In its place, he installed discreet lights behind the decorative finishes to each setback in the facade. This produced a startling chiaroscuro effect across the surface of the building at night, inspiring the artist Georgia O'Keefe to produce one of her most famous paintings.

Daily News Building

location: *New York, USA*

architects: *John Howells and Raymond Hood*

completed: *1930 (as seen today with the addition by Harrison & Abramowitz, 1958)*

Built between 1929 and 1930, the Daily News Building let Raymond Hood and John Howells perfect their approach to skyscraper design, first developed in neo-Gothic in Chicago, but now completely realized in an Art Deco and modern International Style. At 476 feet (145 m) and 36 floors, the Daily News Building was taller than the American Radiator Building (see page 82), completed five years previously, and it eschewed much of the rich ornamentation of that building. Instead, they developed a subtle approach to the design of the skyscraper.

Modern monolith

From a distance, two things stand out from the Daily News Building. First, the immense vertical piers traveling without interruption from ground to crown, stretching and emphasizing the building's height. Second, the irregular setbacks across each facade, creating a jagged, craggy, or sawtooth surface. Both of these effects were deliberate attempts to solve the specific problem of the skyscraper— light and zonal setbacks.

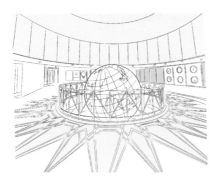

News of the world

Although certainly austere compared with the American Radiator Building or the Chicago Tribune, the Daily News Building still advertised the strength of its proprietor. The lobby had a large black glass, domed ceiling, within which was suspended a colossal globe. Viewable from galleries, it was proposed as a "scientific, educational" feature of the building.

Built without an ornamental crown

Designated a New York City Landmark

A large carved mural above the entrance depicts Manhattan workers under the motif "He made so many of them"

Setbacks

The setbacks on the facade of the Daily News Building are the product of maximizing floor area while conforming to the zoning regulations of New York City. These regulations had been worked up into drawings, showing maximum permissible volumes, by the architectural illustrator Hugh Ferris. Hood and Howells's design was later represented in one of Ferris's drawings—showing a full circle from regulation to resolution.

Vertical emphasis

The vertical stripes of the building are produced by piers of white brickwork. Within these verticals are stacked many thousands of windows, each just large enough for an individual office worker to comfortably open. The spandrels between each window are of brown brick. Viewed close up, these appear finely decorated; from far away, they recede completely.

Chrysler Building

location: *New York, USA*

architects: *William Van Alen and H. Craig Severance*

completed: *1931*

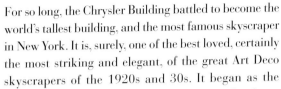

For so long, the Chrysler Building battled to become the world's tallest building, and the most famous skyscraper in New York. It is, surely, one of the best loved, certainly the most striking and elegant, of the great Art Deco skyscrapers of the 1920s and 30s. It began as the brainchild of real-estate developer William H. Reynolds, and eventually it was the result of the desire of Walter Chrysler, founder of the Chrysler automotive company, to bequeath an enduring legacy to his heirs. On completion in 1931, the Chrysler Building was, at 1,046 feet (319 m), the tallest building in the world—for 11 months—until it was eclipsed by the Empire State Building.

Art Deco jewel

A single, stand-alone, setback tower, the Chrysler Building was far from "pioneering" in architectural terms. Yet it remains iconic, not least as a result of the spectacular Art Deco styling of its crown and the many sculptural motifs evident throughout the building, as well as the imitating elements of the Chrysler cars of the 1920s.

Change of form

The architects, originally William Van Alen and H. Craig Severance (although Severance would leave the partnership before the Chrysler was finalized), tried a number of approaches to the crown of the building. These were published as the project proceeded. Various domes were proposed, but in the end, the stack of seven radiating terraced arches, each filled with triangular vaulted windows, receding to a point and spire, all clad in metal, proved the winning formula.

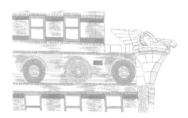

Decorative motifs

The Chrysler is, perhaps, as famous for its decorative motifs as its crown. At the corner of each setback at the top of the tower, massive, stylized metal eagles reach out like gargoyles. Farther down, much closer to street level, the corners of the building are set with gargoyles, modeled as gigantic winged radiator caps. The building's facade is further decorated with stylized automobiles. The crown and additional ornamentation used 29,961 tons of steel.

Interior lobby

The interior is as spectacular as the exterior, and as much a celebration of travel. Using African marble, bronze, and glass, the lobby area is filled with mosaic and mural, displaying industry, technology, and above all, the power of mechanically aided transportation—a celebration of modernity as speed.

Empire State Building

The most famous skyscraper in the world, the Empire State Building was also the tallest for nearly 40 years. Completed in 1931, only 13½ months after construction had begun, the Empire State Building went on to become not only one of the most visited buildings in New York (most visitors to the Empire State Building will go to one of the viewing decks on the 86th or 102nd floors), but one of its most iconic—appearing in newspapers, photographs, movies (not least, *King Kong*, see page 57), paintings, and later television and even video games. The Empire State Building is the epitome of Art Deco design and the great American skyscraper.

location: *New York, USA*
architects: *Shreve, Lamb & Harmon*
completed: *1931*

Race to the sky
The Empire State Building reaches 1,250 feet (381 m) and has 102 floors. Original designs, by the architects Shreve, Lamb & Harmon, proposed a much shorter building, but the Empire State was caught in a "race to the sky," with the contemporary Chrysler (see page 86), and 40 Wall Street. The Chrysler, in particular, pressed ever higher, and only late in the process of design was the final 16-story, 200-foot (61-m) metal crown with mast added.

Assembling the steel frame

Construction of the Empire State utilized the most advanced assembling techniques and detailed negotiations with unionized labor. Using prefabricated steel parts, borrowing techniques from Ford assembly-line manufacture, the structure was completed in eight months. At any one time up to 3,500 workers were operating on the construction. The schedule was so tight that contractors were instructed to start work in March 1930, before final designs had been completed.

Stepped profile

The Empire State was initially modeled by the architects on an earlier building designed in North Carolina. The architects then proceeded to assess the maximum permissible width of each story, according to the 1916 Zoning Resolution.

Using "bug diagrams," the design team worked from top to bottom, creating the stepped profile of the building

Docking station

Above the viewing platform on the 102 floor, the building continues with a 158-foot (48-m) hollow mast. It was originally intended as a "dirigible docking station," a landing platform for zeppelins and blimps. However, due to high winds (up to 40 mph/64 km/h) only one landing was ever made—it lasted 3 minutes.

Rockefeller Center

location: *New York, USA*

architects: *Reinhard & Hofmeister (gen. arch.); Raymond Hood*

completed: *1940*

If the Chrysler (see page 86) is the Art Deco period's most elegant skyscraper, and the Empire State (see page 88) its most iconic, Rockefeller Center is its most sophisticated. A complex that includes 19 buildings, built over nine years, and spread over 22 acres (89,000 m²), the true skyscraper of the Center, designed by Raymond Hood, is 30 Rockefeller Center (or, more colloquially, "30 Rock"), originally known as the RCA Building. In a development of Hood's approach to skyscraper design, 30 Rock uses setbacks and a sharp profile to create the focus for the Center as a whole.

Exterior of 30 Rock

The original proposal for the site was for a new opera house for the Metropolitan Opera company. Unable to sustain the financing, the site was taken over by John D. Rockefeller Jr., financier, philanthropist, and heir to the Standard Oil fortune. Hood was commissioned as lead architect for the complex, and it was his proposal to form a relationship with RCA (Radio Corporation of America) to create a huge media complex.

Sixth Avenue

RCA

Rockefeller Plaza

Rockefeller Plaza

Fifth Avenue

30 Rock (left)

Unlike the Empire State or Chrysler buildings, which had a single office function, the RCA Building was always intended to house a mixture of different studios, auditoria, and media production environments. As a result, the building's cross section produces a fantastic array of different uses, all housed within a uniform exterior.

Inner calm (right)

As part of his Art Deco scheme, Hood ensured that rooftop gardens were established throughout, treating these as the "planting" around a domestic home, adding light and breathable space to the core of the city.

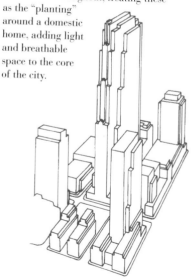

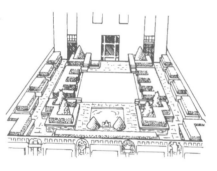

Elevation

The RCA building is a single structure but appears as sections. The main 66-story tower, which reaches 872 feet (266 m), and rises from the eastern part of the base, is flanked by a windowless section in the center, and a short 20-story tower at the western edge of the base. The overall design is a consequence of Hood's adherence to "setback"—yet, curiously, this was entirely for aesthetic effect: because the RCA Building was in the middle of the Center, it wasn't required to follow the 1916 Zoning Resolution.

Introduction

MLC Centre
The strikingly Modernist white forms of the MLC Centre in Sydney, Australia, completed in 1977. Its octagonal tower remains one of the tallest reinforced concrete buildings in the world.

By the mid-nineteenth century, the expertise and materials required to design and construct skyscrapers were within easy reach of every country on the earth. Modern transportation and communication let architects and engineers work across continents, designing buildings on one side of the world and having them constructed on the other. Just as vital to

the skyscraper's spread were the extraction and mass production of new materials, such as iron, steel, concrete, and sheet glass, and the skills required by the modern construction worker in welding, riveting, piling, and concrete formwork. Today, we take all this for granted, but it is hard not to marvel at the speed with which such developments spread across the globe.

Royal Liver Building

location: *Liverpool, UK*
architect: *Walter Aubrey Thomas*
completed: *1911*

Commissioned as the new headquarters for the Royal Liver Assurance company, the Royal Liver Building officially opened on July 19, 1911. One of the earliest buildings to be constructed from reinforced concrete, it is testament to the economic and global prowess of the port of Liverpool at the height of its power in the early twentieth century. Standing at more than 300 feet (91 m) high with 13 main floors, it was the tallest building in Great Britain until the 1960s. Since 2004, the building has been the centerpiece of the UNESCO World Heritage Site that comprises Liverpool's famous waterfront and docks.

International inspiration

The progressive design of this early skyscraper is said to have inspired other buildings all over the world, including the Manhattan Municipal Building in New York, the Seven Sisters in Moscow (see page 106), and the former Custom House in Shanghai, Liverpool's sister city.

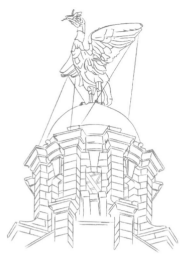

Innovation (below)

The building demonstrates the first use in Great Britain of the reinforced concrete frame on this scale—controversial at the time, because many believed it would never work. This new material and method of construction pushed the heights of the buildings ever taller at the beginning of the twentieth century, although their exteriors—in this case, a skin of granite—retained many of the classical features of former masonry structures.

Liver birds (above)

Atop each of the clock towers are copper sculptures of the mythical liver bird—a symbol of the city—designed by the London-based German wood-carver Carl Bernard Bartels. According to local legend, the male and female pair stand guard over Liverpool, and were they ever to fly away, the city would flood.

Mighty clock

Housed in the pair of six-story clock towers that crown the Royal Liver Building are the first electrically driven clocks in Great Britain. With a diameter of 25 feet (7.6 m), their faces are 2 feet (0.6 m) larger than the clock that tops Elizabeth Tower at Westminster in London (better known as Big Ben, after the bell inside).

KBC Tower

Constructed on a prime site in central Antwerp and completed in stages between 1929 and 1932 to an original height of 287 feet (87 m), the Boerentoren—or KBC Tower—was the tallest building in Europe throughout the 1930s, and it remains the second highest building in Antwerp. Three architects were appointed to oversee the overall design. Emiel Van Averbeke, the city architect, was chief adviser on behalf of the municipality, with Jan Vanhoenacker appointed builder and Jos Smolderen responsible for the interior and facade. The tower was designed as a multifunctional building, containing a bank and commercial properties at street level and apartments above. It was converted to offices throughout in the late 1960s.

location: *Antwerp, Belgium*
architects: *Emiel Van Averbeke,*
Jan Vanhoenacker, and Jos Smolderen
completed: *1932*

Farmers' Tower

The first skyscraper in Europe was originally known as the Boerentoren, or Farmers' Tower, after the farmers' collective that invested in its construction. The current tenant is the KBC banking and insurance company, from which the building gets its official title.

Modern design

The building's clean vertical lines
represented a minor revolution in the
modern aesthetics of tall buildings in
Europe, which by the 1930s were shaking
off the cloak of classicism that struggled
to fit the skyscraper's tall frame. The
detailing also followed suit, as seen in the
eight bronze sculptures above the main
entrance, designed in a Modernist style
by sculptor Arthur Pierre.

Steel frame (below)

The tower achieved its height through the
use of a lightweight steel frame weighing
3,747 tons and assembled by the firm Demag
from Duisburg, using
nearly half a million rivets
and 180,000 bolts. The
exterior was faced in
15,000 square feet
(1,390 m²) of white
Burgundian stone.

Growing taller

In 1954, an antenna was added to the
the building, raising its height to 369 feet
(112 m)—a strategy often employed by
skyscraper builders and owners to boost
their vital statistics. Then, in 1976, the roof
was raised, achieving the current roof height
of 314 feet (96 m).

Senate House

location: *London, UK*
architect: *Charles Holden*
completed: *1937*

Designed by the British architect Charles Holden, Senate House was the centerpiece of the University of London's new campus in the heart of historic Bloomsbury. Because the superstructure was intended to contain various university offices and a new library, it had to be constructed using a steel frame to support the weight of the book stacks. The exterior walls were built using load-bearing Cornish granite at the base and engineering bricks faced in Portland stone above. In London, Portland stone had long been Holden's material of choice for its distinctive weathering, which he appreciated greatly and encouraged in the way he detailed specific cuts to the stonework—so that the building could "wash its own face."

Dubious associations

Senate House's monumental appearance has divided opinion since the beginning, with an austerity that has invited some dubious associations. Hitler supposedly earmarked the building for his headquarters upon a successful invasion of Great Britain; it also inspired the writer George Orwell's Ministry of Truth in his novel *Nineteen Eighty-Four*, and featured in the movie adaptation of the book.

Klauder's Cathedral of Learning

Although Holden's original design incorporated two towers, the final design had just one 210-foot (64-m) tower, inspired by the cathedral towers of Europe and seen as a twentieth-century "Cathedral of Learning," akin to Charles Zeller Klauder's 1926 educational skyscraper at the University of Pittsburgh.

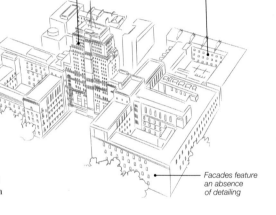

Upper levels are set back

Four courts were intended for balance, although only three were eventually completed

Facades feature an absence of detailing

Massing

The principle behind the building's form was massing, whereby the assembly and setting back of cubic masses creates an effect of monumentality and a strong sense of proportion, scale, and elevation. A close inspection reveals the architect's painstaking attention to detail to achieve this effect.

Traditional versus modern

The building's design straddled the huge shift from the traditional (the proportional arrangement of the masses and windows, for example) to the modern (the unadorned geometric volumes and sheer scale). Holden declared that he was not traditional enough to please the traditionalists, and not modern enough to please the Modernists either.

The Shard

Located over London Bridge Station in Southwark, London, the Shard was conceived by the Italian architect Renzo Piano, and at 1,016 feet (310 m)—or 95 stories—was the tallest building in Western Europe on completion. Lightness and transparency were the key principles behind the design, which can be seen not only in its pointed, shardlike form but also in its use of glazing. The building is clad in 11,000 panels of double-layer glass, and this glass was specially designed to reflect natural light, giving the building a uniquely mercurial, ethereal quality.

location: *London, UK*
architect: *Renzo Piano*
completed: *2013*

Complex site
The Shard occupies a tight and complex site above both mainline and underground railroad stations. Due to these constraints, the foundations were constructed as the skyscraper was erected, meaning construction went up and down from the street level simultaneously.

A city in a building (right)

The Shard combines reinforced concrete and steel: a concrete core, surrounded and topped by a lightweight steel frame to support the floors. The core provides strength and rigidity while the steel frame is designed to provide flexibility of up to 20 inches (51 cm) in high winds. For its 72 habitable floors, the building was designed to accommodate a range of different functions that might typically be found on a London street. These include offices, a hotel, apartments, restaurants, and public spaces. Floors 4–28 are dedicated to office space, to benefit from the larger floor areas lower down.

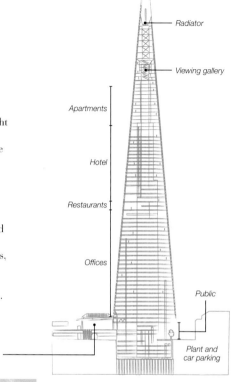

Radiator

Viewing gallery

Apartments

Hotel

Restaurants

Offices

Public

Plant and car parking

Approach

Inspired by history

The Shard overlooks the Pool of London, the stretch of the Thames River between Tower Bridge and London Bridge. It is where sailing ships from all over the globe once berthed to dispense their goods against a backdrop of the City of London, with its dozens of churches designed by Sir Christopher Wren. The ships' masts and Wren's spires inspired the Shard's form.

Torre Velasca

location: *Milan, Italy*
architect: *BBPR*
completed: *1958*

Idiosyncratic icon
The tower's design has attracted both positive and negative attention. Although some have branded the "skyscraper with suspenders" as the ugliest building in Europe, it is now protected as a historical building.

Rising 348 feet (106 m) over a residential quarter of the historic city of Milan, the distinctly modern concrete form of the Torre Velasca was, in fact, inspired by the past. Its design by the BBPR partnership (architects Gian Luigi Banfi, Lodovico Barbiano di Belgiojoso, Enrico Peressutti, and Ernesto Nathan Rogers) was based on the medieval fortresses and watchtowers that once rose above ancient Italian towns, with slim bases and wider platforms that cantilevered out from the top. The top-heavy Torre Velasca follows this principle but takes it to the extreme by employing untreated cast and precast reinforced concrete as its primary material.

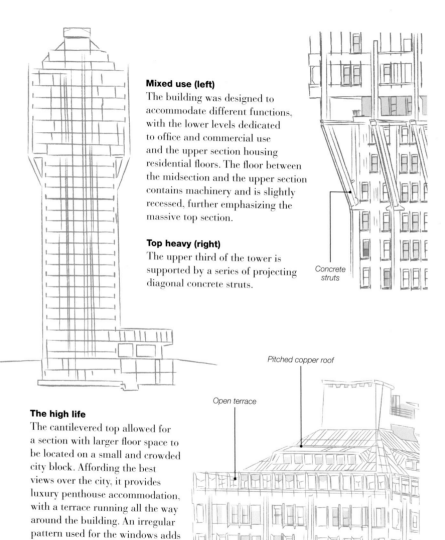

Mixed use (left)

The building was designed to accommodate different functions, with the lower levels dedicated to office and commercial use and the upper section housing residential floors. The floor between the midsection and the upper section contains machinery and is slightly recessed, further emphasizing the massive top section.

Top heavy (right)

The upper third of the tower is supported by a series of projecting diagonal concrete struts.

Concrete struts

Pitched copper roof

Open terrace

The high life

The cantilevered top allowed for a section with larger floor space to be located on a small and crowded city block. Affording the best views over the city, it provides luxury penthouse accommodation, with a terrace running all the way around the building. An irregular pattern used for the windows adds visual interest.

Terrazza Martini Tower

location: *Genoa, Italy*
architect: *Marcello Piacentini*
completed: *1940*

Designed in 1935 for the Martini & Rossi Company by Mussolini's favored architect, Marcello Piacentini, the Terrazza Martini Tower was the tallest building in Europe until 1952, the year the Kotelnicheskaya Embankment apartments were completed in Moscow (see page 107). Mussolini himself had long been fascinated by skyscrapers and the engineering prowess of the United States. Although this 31-story skyscraper towered 380 feet (116 m) over the city of Genoa, its pared-back design embraced the Fascist spatial planning inspired by the imperial pomp of the Roman Empire.

Shifting perspectives
The architecture and planning of the tower were carefully choreographed so that its impact changed when viewed from its immediate surroundings in the Piazza Dante, compared with the wider context of the ancient city, whose streetscape frames differing views of the tower.

Commercial power (right)

For centuries, the skylines of Italian cities have been pierced by towers constructed by wealthy merchant families eager to promote their stature. The Terrazza Martini Tower continued this tradition by building tall in celebration of commercial success.

Palazzo della Civiltà Italiana (left)

Many Modernist architects advocated a break with the past, but in Italy, Modernist architecture was known as "rationalism." It borrowed from the proportions and massing of Classical architecture while dispensing with the ornamentation—a stripped-back classicism that reached its apogee with the design of the EUR— the Esposizione Universale Roma—an interbellum neighborhood of Rome.

Striped skin

The materiality of the tower is further defined by a stone exterior at its base and horizontal bands of brick and stone higher up—intended to echo the striped stonework of Genoa's traditional buildings.

Stalin's Seven Sisters

location: *Moscow, Russia*

architects: *various*

completed: *1957*

Kotelnicheskaya Embankment high-rises
Following Stalin's death in 1953, the Seven Sisters were criticized for their excesses and inefficiency, and under the new leadership of Nikita Khrushchev, Stalinist architecture came to an end.

Starting in 1947, Stalin commissioned seven high-rises—the Seven Sisters, or Stalinskie Vysotki (Stalin's high-rises)—that were designed by a number of different architects and completed over the following decade. They both transformed and defined Moscow's skyline. The buildings were overengineered using massive steel frames that were far heavier than they needed to be. In the case of the Red Gates Administrative Building, the steel frame was constructed with a deliberate lean to counter the defrosting of the soil after winter, but the engineers miscalculated and the building retains its lean to this day.

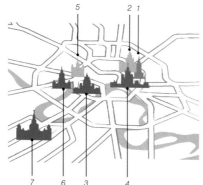

Building locations

The Seven Sisters from shortest to tallest are: Leningradskaya Hotel (1); Red Gates Administrative Building (2); Ministry of Foreign Affairs (3); Kotelnicheskaya Embankment apartments (4); Kudrinskaya Square Building (5); Hotel Ukraina (6); and (7) Moscow State University. An eighth, the Zaryadye Administrative Building, would have topped them all at 902 feet (275 m), but it was never built.

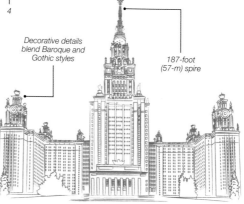

Decorative details blend Baroque and Gothic styles

187-foot (57-m) spire

Stalin's style

The distinctive decorative style that unites all seven of these buildings is known as Socialist Classicism. It was the architectural accompaniment to Socialist Realism in art, an official style sanctioned by the Communist Party and its leader.

Big sister

Standing 790 feet (240 m) high in its central section—including a spire topped with a five-pointed star—the 36-story Moscow State University designed by Lev Rudnev is the tallest of the Seven Sisters. It was the tallest building in Europe until 1990, when it was surpassed by the 843-foot-high (257 m) Messeturm in Frankfurt.

Palace of Culture and Science

location: *Warsaw, Poland*

architect: *Lev Rudnev*

completed: *1955*

Rising from the ruins

After World War II, it was decided to reconstruct Warsaw, with the exception of the Palace of Culture and Science. At 778 feet (237 m), its presence over the rebuilt city sent a clear political message.

A gift from the Soviet Union to the people of Poland, the 42-story Joseph Stalin Palace of Culture and Science was designed by Lev Rudnev, the Russian architect who also designed the tallest of Stalin's Seven Sisters—Moscow State University (page 107). The Polish skyscraper was based on the plans for an unbuilt eighth skyscraper, so is consequently sometimes referred to as the Eighth Sister. As with its Moscow siblings, the Palace was built using an over-engineered steel frame cloaked in a Socialist Classical exterior, but with some Polish features.

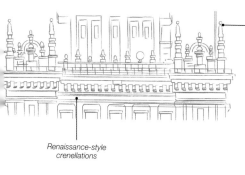

Pointed pinnacles reference traditional Polish style

Renaissance-style crenellations

Troubled memory (below)

References to Stalin were erased from the building after the despised leader's death, but the building continues to divide opinion between those who accept it as a memory of a troubled past and those who find that memory too painful and would rather the entire building be erased.

Local context (left)

Having traveled around Poland to conduct design research, Rudnev incorporated many Polish references in his Socialist Classical monument. Decorative details inspired by the Renaissance architecture of Krakow and Zamosc can be seen on the building's exterior, including the pointed pinnacles along the parapets.

Public palace

The principal function of the Palace of Culture and Science was to serve the public, housing museums, theaters, movie theaters, educational and scientific institutions, sporting venues, and a conference hall that not only hosted political meetings but also a concert by the Rolling Stones in 1967.

BMW Headquarters

location: *Munich, Germany*

architect: *Karl Schwanzer*

completed: *1972*

Designed by the Austrian architect Karl Schwanzer, a former student of the great Brazilian architect Oscar Niemeyer, the innovative BMW Headquarters building made an indelible impression on the skyline of the ancient Bavarian city of Munich when it was constructed in the 1970s. The tower rises 326 feet (99.5 m), just within the city's building regulations. These were established in 1968 to make sure that no building would exceed 328 feet (100 m), slightly more than the height of the Frauenkirche, the city's imposing fifteenth-century cathedral.

Modern landmark

Erected next to the Olympiapark built for the 1972 Olympic Games, the tower was completed by the same date, although it was not officially inaugurated until May 1973.

Suspended construction

The four interconnected cylindrical volumes are hung from a reinforced concrete core and massive steel framework that can be seen protruding from the top. Despite weighing 18, 518 tons, the cylinders are suspended above the ground. This innovative method of construction meant that not only could each floor be constructed on the ground and lifted hydraulically into place, but construction could aso start from the top and work its way down.

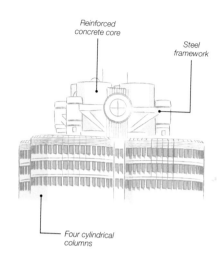

Reinforced concrete core

Steel framework

Four cylindrical columns

Museum (above)

Standing apart from the main tower is the low-rise building also designed by Schwanzer for the BMW Museum. As with the main tower, the design of the museum was inspired by a motor engine; it takes the form of a cylinder head.

Split facade (right)

The distinctive sculptural form of the building, comprising four conjoined cylinders, was inspired by the combustion chambers inside motor engines. Cloverleaf in plan, the 18 stories of offices are divided by one recessed plant floor above the 11th story, giving the building's profile a sense of lightness and visual separation.

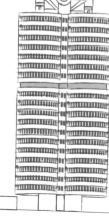

Museum

Ryōunkaku

As the tallest building in Japan in its day, the Ryōunkaku marked a milestone in the construction of tall buildings in Asia. Japan was the first Asian nation to adopt and adapt Western principles of construction and design, and the Ryōunkaku was the first Western-style skyscraper in that country, designed by the engineer William Burton and completed at the end of the nineteenth century. At 12 stories and 225 feet (69 m) high, the building towered above the Asakusa district, and its views and stores became a major attraction for local residents.

location: *Tokyo, Japan*
architect: *William Kinnimond Burton*
completed: *1890*

Western influence

Despite the building's alien appearance, the construction techniques and materials were conventional, using an octagonal timber frame and brick exterior. The style was an eclectic mix of the Western architectural styles popular in Japan at the time.

Seismic victim (right)

Japan's volatile seismic conditions wrought havoc on this tall structure. After tremors had weakened the building in 1894, the building was reinforced with steel, but even this could not withstand the Great Kanto earthquake of 1923, which razed much of the city and left the Ryōunkaku irreparably damaged.

Technological innovation (below)

Skyscrapers have always pushed the boundaries of innovation. For Japan, the Ryōunkaku embodied modernity with the country's first two electric elevators, designed by Ichisuke Fujioka, the founder of Toshiba, as well as electric lighting on every floor and around the observation decks.

Urban panorama (left)

The skyscraper has played a vital role in changing our perception of and relationship with cities. Buildings like the Ryōunkaku let the public view their city from above for the very first time—from specially designed observation decks on the top three floors—an experience that had a big impact on art, literature, and photography.

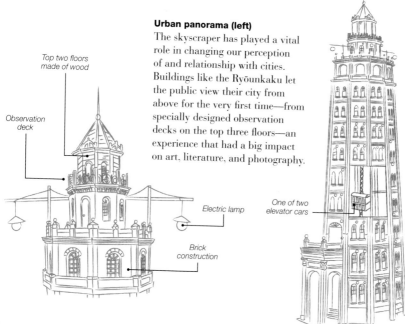

Top two floors made of wood

Observation deck

Electric lamp

Brick construction

One of two elevator cars

Park Hotel (Shanghai)

location: *Shanghai, China*

architect: *László Hudec*

completed: *1934*

Designed by a Hungarian architect for a Chinese financial consortium, the Joint Savings Society, this head offices and five-star hotel was Asia's tallest building when completed in 1934, and it remained China's tallest building until the 1980s. The skyscraper comprised two parts: the 22-story tower at the front and a lower section extending to the rear. To prevent this huge steel-frame structure from sinking into Shanghai's alluvial soil, the skyscraper was built on a reinforced raft, 24 feet (7.3 m) deep, and supported on 400 wooden piles, each 150 feet (46 m) in length.

All mod cons

This modern skyscraper boasted the latest luxuries and technologies, including air-conditioning and five express elevators—two for services and three for guests. Visitors could also dine in the fashionable grill room on the 14th floor, which featured velvet curtains, a gold ceiling, and was lined in Austrian walnut with silver inlay.

Radiator Building (left)

The distinctive vertical detailing, dark brown brickwork, and stepped profile was directly inspired by Raymond Hood's Radiator Building in New York (see page 82), which Hudec had recently visited.

Exploiting the building regulations

In Shanghai, the building regulations constrained a building's height to one-and-a-half times the width of the road it fronted. The Park Hotel overlooked the racecourse, so it avoided these restrictions.

Top

Middle

Base

275 feet (84 m) tall

22 stories

Classical composition (above)

Despite its modern appearance, the hotel is arranged like a classical column, with a clearly defined base, middle, and top. The base comprises the first three floors, which are faced in black marble and arranged horizontally. The middle section, vertically arranged and faced in brown brick, comprises the 4th through 14th floors. The top section tapers to an octagonal observatory.

Bank of China Tower

location: *Hong Kong, China*

architect: *I. M. Pei*

completed: *1990*

Designed by the Pritzker Prize-winning Chinese-American architect Ieoh Ming Pei, the Bank of China Tower in Hong Kong is perhaps his most famous and innovative work. Standing 1,205 feet (367 m) tall in the heart of downtown Hong Kong, the office building was the tallest skyscraper outside North America when completed. Designed on a tight budget and for a restricted site, the efficient steel framework is functionally expressed through the triangulated exterior, which rises in four triangular vertical shafts from a square plan that is divided into four quadrants.

An inauspicious design?

Followers of local beliefs have long been critical of Pei's masterpiece, with feng shui masters claiming that the building's site, form, and symbolism violate their philosophy's principles of harmony. Sharp corners resemble knife blades, while the Xs formed by the visible triangular framework recall the symbol for a death sentence.

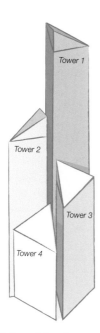

Tower 1

Tower 2

Tower 3

Tower 4

Efficiency (above)

Inspired by bamboo as a symbol of strength, growth, and prosperity, the structural efficiency of this triangular solution was also materially and economically efficient, using half the steel of an average building of this size, and, therefore, costing considerably less.

Typhoon resistance (below)

Due to the typhoons that frequently strike Hong Kong, the tower's triangular forms were designed to withstand wind loads at least double those experienced in New York. Five massive columns—one at the center and the others at each corner of the building—carry its weight and offer further wind resistance.

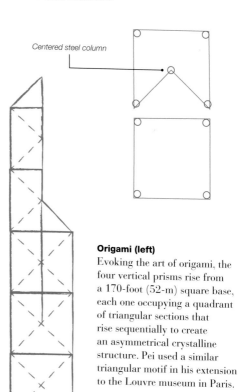

Centered steel column

Origami (left)

Evoking the art of origami, the four vertical prisms rise from a 170-foot (52-m) square base, each one occupying a quadrant of triangular sections that rise sequentially to create an asymmetrical crystalline structure. Pei used a similar triangular motif in his extension to the Louvre museum in Paris.

Ryugyong Hotel

location:
*Pyongyang,
North Korea*

architect:
*Baikdoosan
Architects &
Engineers*

completed:
*unfinished
(2018)*

Perhaps one of the least known or visited skyscrapers in the world is the unfinished Ryugyong Hotel in the North Korean capital of Pyongyang. The 105-story reinforced concrete structure's futuristic pretensions began in the 1980s, but construction stalled in the 1990s with the collapse of the Soviet Union. The 1,080-foot-high (329 m) building was designed to be a mixed-use development housing the world's tallest hotel and was completely glazed in 2011. However, in its unfinished state, it is instead the world's tallest unoccupied skyscraper.

Protracted construction

The construction costs of this behemoth are estimated to be up to $750 million, or 2 percent of GDP. Construction was halted by escalating costs and simultaneously worsening economic conditions in the 1990s, but it resumed in 2008 with the help, perhaps fittingly, of Egyptian investors.

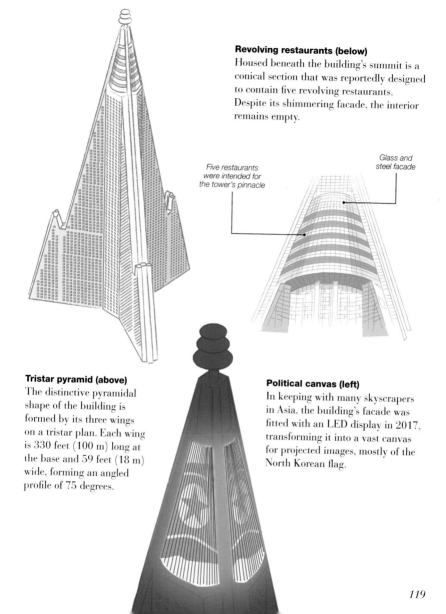

Revolving restaurants (below)
Housed beneath the building's summit is a conical section that was reportedly designed to contain five revolving restaurants. Despite its shimmering facade, the interior remains empty.

Five restaurants were intended for the tower's pinnacle

Glass and steel facade

Tristar pyramid (above)
The distinctive pyramidal shape of the building is formed by its three wings on a tristar plan. Each wing is 330 feet (100 m) long at the base and 59 feet (18 m) wide, forming an angled profile of 75 degrees.

Political canvas (left)
In keeping with many skyscrapers in Asia, the building's facade was fitted with an LED display in 2017, transforming it into a vast canvas for projected images, mostly of the North Korean flag.

Petronas Towers

When completed, the Petronas Towers usurped Chicago's Willis Tower (formerly the Sears Tower, see page 166) as the world's tallest building. Designed by the Argentine-American architect César Pelli to reflect Malaysia's booming economy during the 1990s, the 1,483-foot (452-m) twin structures also embodied the local cultural context, with a geometry defined by Islamic traditions, and and interior decoration inspired by local handicrafts and traditional *songket* (weaving). The multifaceted exterior walls were clad in 33,000 panels of stainless steel and 55,000 panels of glass.

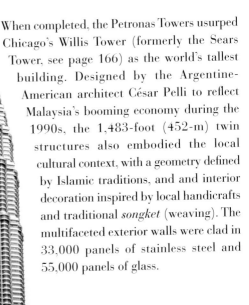

location: *Kuala Lumpur, Malaysia*
architect: *César Pelli*
completed: *1999*

Tapered design
The 88 stories of each tower above ground are stepped at five intervals, with increasingly tapered walls that create the heightened impression of elevation toward the pinnacle.

Islamic plan (right)

The plan of each floor derives from the unifying and harmonious Islamic principle of two interlocking squares to create an eight-pointed star, with each corner infilled with a circular pattern. The combination of and relationship between perpendicular and radial outlines creates distinctive interiors and defines the building's elaborate exterior.

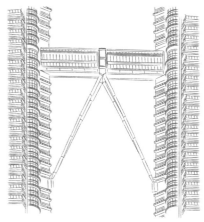

Skybridge

The conspicuous skybridge that connects the buildings at the 41st and 42nd floors serves no structural function. However, visually, conceptually, and practically, it unites the two towers and serves as a vital part of the buildings' evacuation strategy.

Race to the top (right)

As an incentive to complete the building in under six years, the two towers were constructed by different consortia—one Japanese and one South Korean, with a financial reward for the first to finish. South Korea, builders of Tower 2, won.

Jin Mao Tower

location: *Shanghai, China*

architect: *Skidmore, Owings & Merrill (SOM)*

completed: *1999*

When it was announced in the early 1990s that the neglected industrial area on the eastern banks of Shanghai's Huangpu River was to become the new financial heart of this once-fabled metropolis, the brakes were off in a race to construct what has become one of the most breathtaking urban skylines. The early centerpiece in this exceptional panorama was the Jin Mao Tower, a shimmering futuristic pagoda, 1,380 feet tall, and designed by Skidmore, Owings & Merrill.

Construction

Due to its complex interior, shape, and setting, the tower comprises an octagonal reinforced concrete core surrounded by eight concrete columns and eight steel columns connected to the core by massive trusses. An absence of bedrock in a seismically active and typhoon-prone region required a foundation of 1,062 steel piles driven 274 feet (85 m) into the soil that is topped by a 13-foot (4-m) concrete raft.

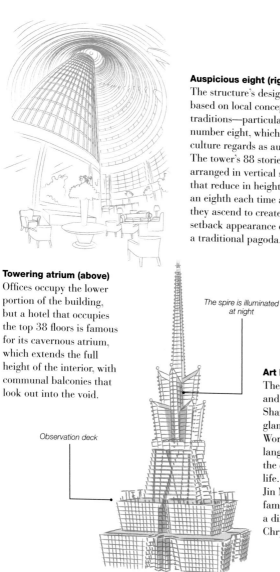

Auspicious eight (right)

The structure's design was based on local concepts and traditions—particularly the number eight, which Chinese culture regards as auspicious. The tower's 88 stories are arranged in vertical sections that reduce in height by an eighth each time as they ascend to create the setback appearance of a traditional pagoda.

Towering atrium (above)

Offices occupy the lower portion of the building, but a hotel that occupies the top 38 floors is famous for its cavernous atrium, which extends the full height of the interior, with communal balconies that look out into the void.

Observation deck

The spire is illuminated at night

Art Deco icon (left)

The glistening stainless steel and glass exterior also recalls Shanghai's more recent and glamorous past, when, before World War II, the flamboyant language of Art Deco defined the city's artistic and cultural life. As a modern Asian icon, Jin Mao rivals New York's famous Art Deco icon from a different generation—the Chrysler Building (page 86).

85 Sky Tower

Designed by local architects, C. Y. Lee & Partners, and US firm Hellmuth, Obata & Kassabaum (HOK), the 85 Sky Tower (previously known as the T&C Tower) is one of the most idiosyncratic skyscrapers of its generation. Upon completion, it was the tallest building in Taiwan. Occupying a rectangular site, the building appears to stand on two legs that support a main body in the center rising to 1,140 feet (347 m). The void between these solid elements creates a strong visual impact.

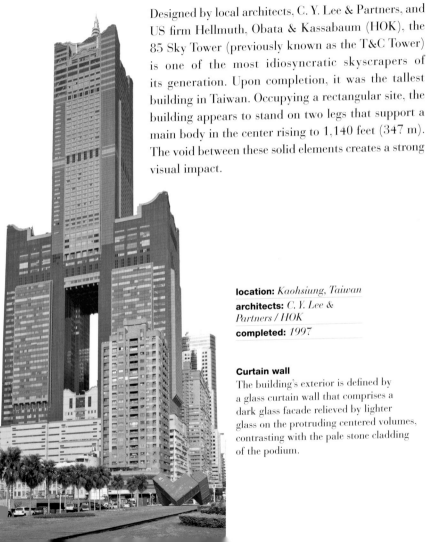

location: *Kaohsiung, Taiwan*
architects: *C. Y. Lee & Partners / HOK*
completed: *1997*

Curtain wall
The building's exterior is defined by a glass curtain wall that comprises a dark glass facade relieved by lighter glass on the protruding centered volumes, contrasting with the pale stone cladding of the podium.

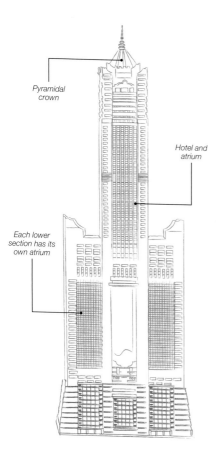

Pyramidal crown

Hotel and atrium

Each lower section has its own atrium

Podium (above)

The whole building stands on a rectangular podium designed to accommodate a tunnel that allows circulation at street level. It also houses the eight reinforced concrete cores, which—combined with a steel frame— provide the building's structural integrity.

Towering atria

Two separate "prongs" rise to meet the main body in the center of the tower, which houses a hotel that extends from the 38th to the 70th floors. An internal atrium extends from the 45th to the 83rd floors, one of the tallest atria in the world. Each lower section also contains a multistory atrium, letting light penetrate deep into the building.

Chinese characteristics

The building possesses various Chinese characteristics, but none more conspicuous than its distinctive shape, which is an abstract interpretation of the first Chinese character (*gao*) of the city's name, Kaohsiung. *Gao* also means "tall."

Commerce Court North

location: *Toronto, Canada*

architects: *York & Sawyer / Darling & Pearson*

completed: *1931*

Designed as the opulent headquarters of the Canadian Bank of Commerce, the Commerce Building was Canada's first skyscraper. It was designed by architects York & Sawyer, who specialize in bank design, in partnership with a local firm, Darling & Pearson. The 34-story structure was not only the tallest building in Canada at the time, but was also the tallest in the British Empire until 1962, when it was overtaken by the neighboring CIBC Tower. Its limestone exterior now sits nestled among taller glass-fronted structures.

Elder statesman
In the 1970s, a further three skyscrapers, designed by I. M. Pei, were built adjacent to the 1931 building, thereby creating the Commerce Court complex in downtown Toronto—and a new name for the old bank headquarters—to match the corresponding Commerce Court East, West, and South.

Steel-frame structure (right)

As with most skyscrapers of its age, the Canadian Bank of Commerce headquarters achieved its 476-foot (145 m) height with a steel-and-concrete frame, that was then clad in limestone.

Ornamentation (left)

The building's architectural style reveals its turn-of-the-century origins—when the symbolic Neoclassical or neo-Romanesque detailing that adorned so many banks and public institutions was giving way to the structural logic and visual rationalization of Modernism.

Public access (right)

Being the tallest tower in Canada in its time, an observation deck was installed. It encircles the building and runs behind the 16 giant bearded faces that stare out over the city from just beneath the building's parapet. The deck is no longer open to the public.

Martinelli Building

When completed in the 1930s, the Martinelli Building (or Predio Martinelli) was the tallest structure in Brazil; it remained so until after World War II and the completion of the nearby Altino Arantes Building (see page 134), completed just over a decade later. It was added to throughout its lifetime, and now stands at 427 feet (130 m). Built by Giuseppe Martinelli, an Italian immigrant who became a highly successful Brazilian businessman, the eponymous skyscraper was constructed in concrete and clad in stone and brick in the Beaux-Arts style.

location: *São Paulo, Brazil*
architect: *Giuseppe Martinelli*
completed: *1934*

Decline and revival

Despite its opulent origins, the building fell into disrepair in the 1960s, attracting squatters and various criminal activities. The situation was so bad by the mid-1970s that the building was purchased by the municipality and restored. It now houses the Departments of Municipal Housing and Planning.

Staggered construction

The original design was conceived in the early 1920s and comprised a 12-story building, which was then extended in stages. By 1928, it was 20 stories; when completed six years later, it had reached 30 stories (two below ground).

Classical composition

Classically inspired and in the Beaux-Arts style, the building's composition comprises a strong horizontally arranged base, a vertically arranged midsection, and an ornate top section with a small pavilion and terrace at the pinnacle, faced in pink stone.

Ornamented upper floors

Pavilion

Hands-on architect (below)

Martinelli, the building's flamboyant architect, is said to have been directly involved in the building's construction, reviving his former experience in Italy as a bricklayer and delighting in teaching his trade to young apprentices. When complete, he was reputedly so proud of his building that he lived and worked on the top floors. The story also goes that he installed himself here to quash local fears that such a tall building would collapse.

Street-level commercial premises

Edificio Kavanagh

location: *Buenos Aires, Argentina*

architects: *Gregorio Sánchez, Ernesto Lagos, Luis María de la Torre*

completed: *1936*

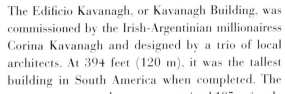

The Edificio Kavanagh, or Kavanagh Building, was commissioned by the Irish-Argentinian millionairess Corina Kavanagh and designed by a trio of local architects. At 394 feet (120 m), it was the tallest building in South America when completed. The skyscraper contained 105 uniquely planned apartments, and Kavanagh kept the largest of them (occupying the whole of the 14th floor) for herself. Determinedly modern for its time, the rational and unadorned style of the building clearly reflected the shift away from Classicism that was occurring in the 1930s.

Innovation

The Kavanagh embraced innovation and broke various records. Not only was it the world's tallest reinforced concrete structure when completed, but it was constructed in a record-breaking 14 months. It was also the first air-conditioned building in the country and among the earliest to boast underground parking, an internal swimming pool, modern plumbing, an internal telephone system—even cold storage for furs!

Modern style (left)

The building's architectural style is displayed principally in the rational composition of simple and stepped geometric volumes that rise to a towering summit on a symmetrically arranged whole. A lack of ornamentation allows clean, continuous vertical lines to heighten the sense of elevation.

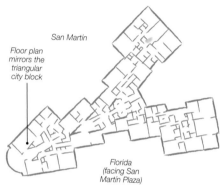

San Martín

Floor plan mirrors the triangular city block

Florida
(facing San Martín Plaza)

Slender structure (right)

The building's slim profile and reinforced concrete structure allowed for a tall yet lightweight building, bound by two diverging streets—San Martín and Florida.

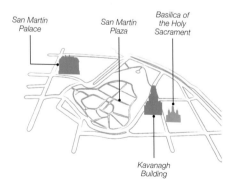

San Martín Palace

San Martín Plaza

Basilica of the Holy Sacrament

Kavanagh Building

Architecture of revenge

Prior to the building's construction, Kavanagh had a love affair with one of the sons of the aristocratic Anchorena family, whose family home was the San Martín Palace. However, his mother ended the union, disapproving of the "nouveau riche" Kavanagh. It is said that Kavanagh's only brief to the architects, therefore, was to block the views of the Anchorena family's private mausoleum, now the Basilica of the Holy Sacrament.

Central do Brasil

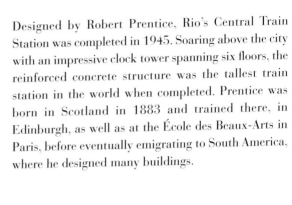

Designed by Robert Prentice, Rio's Central Train Station was completed in 1945. Soaring above the city with an impressive clock tower spanning six floors, the reinforced concrete structure was the tallest train station in the world when completed. Prentice was born in Scotland in 1883 and trained there, in Edinburgh, as well as at the École des Beaux-Arts in Paris, before eventually emigrating to South America, where he designed many buildings.

location: *Rio de Janeiro, Brazil*

architect: *Robert Russell Prentice*

completed: *1945*

Mid-century icon

Centro do Brasil was built on the same site as an original station that dated back to the 1850s. The architectural language and bright plastered exterior of the new structure was conspicuously modern, eschewing the often overt and, by then, seemingly dreary neo-Classicism typical of so many late nineteenth-century railroad termini around the world.

Modern materials (right)

Conceived with efficiency in mind, the exterior exudes rational principles of construction and modern design to aid the efficient circulation of large numbers of passengers into, out of, and through the building to the platforms, while the reinforced concrete allows for bright, spacious interiors.

The giant clock has a diameter of 65 feet (20 m)

Architectural language

The building can be read as a series of horizontal and vertical elements that differentiate between various functions. The asymmetrical seven-story main building containing offices and ticket hall is horizontally composed, with ribbon windows that are interrupted by the vertical fenestration in the center of the building that marks the entrance.

Clock tower

The 443-foot (135-m) tower, with its strong vertical lines and crowning four-sided white Art Deco clock, is deliberately designed to provide a physical and visual contrast—it is stepped toward the top to accentuate the building's height and to create an overall sense of proportion. It remains an iconic part of the Rio skyline.

Altino Arantes Building

Changing identity
The Edifício do Banespa was renamed the Altino Arantes Building in the 1960s, in honor of the bank's first president and President of the State of São Paulo, who died in 1965. Although perhaps still best known by this name, it was renamed the Farol Santander in 2018.

Standing at 528 feet (162 m) tall, the 35-story Altino Arantes Building broke records as the world's tallest reinforced concrete structure. Construction began in September 1939 with the 46-foot (14-m) piles, but it was delayed by World War II, and the building was not completed until June 27, 1947. The stepped form and accentuated verticality of the fenestration paid homage to the Empire State Building (see page 88) in New York, Brazilian architect Plínio Botelho do Amaral's inspiration. The tower was designed as the headquarters of the Bank of the State of São Paulo (Banespa).

location: *São Paulo, Brazil*

architect: *Plínio Botelho do Amaral*

completed: *1947*

Viewing platform

35 stories

1,119 windows

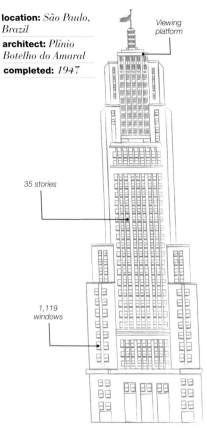

Material finishes (above)
As a state bank's headquarters, little expense was spared on fitting the tower out with the best materials, fixtures, and fittings. The facade facing the main street is covered in more than 20,000 bright white porcelain tiles, the entrance is lined in white marble, many interiors are lined in Carrara marble from Italy, and the parquet wood floors are made of ipe and jacaranda.

Viewing deck
In keeping with its deference to the Empire State Building, the Altino Arantes Building was given a public viewing platform at its top. The deck is accessed by means of 14 elevators— or 900 steps.

Record breaker
Not only was this the world's tallest reinforced concrete structure, upon completion in 1947 the tower became the tallest skyscraper outside the United States. It was the tallest in São Paulo for nearly 20 years.

Mutual Heights

location: *Cape Town, South Africa*

architect: *Louw & Louw*

completed: *1940*

Mutual Heights was designed by Louw & Louw, with Fred Glennie and Ivan Mitford-Barberton, to be the ambitious and glamorous new home of the long-established South Africa Mutual Life Assurance Society. At 276 feet (84 m), it was the tallest building in South Africa on its inauguration and the tallest modern building on the continent (the Pyramids in Egypt are considerably taller; see page 14), beating off the growing number of skyscrapers in the rival city of Johannesburg, including the Anstey's Building, Lewis & Marks, Escom House, and Chrysler House.

Bending the rules

The height of buildings in Cape Town was limited not by any unit of measurement but by the number of floors, which were capped at ten. To achieve their desired height, the architects therefore designed a particularly generous floor-to-floor height of at least 16 feet (5 m).

Ziggurat

The building's distinctive form mirrored many early modern skyscrapers, being composed of a series of stepped volumes that reduced in size as they reached the summit. The ziggurat model was also another way to circumvent local building regulations and achieve extra height.

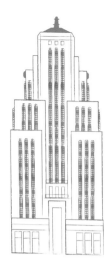

Triangular windows

The unconventional protruding windows with their Modernist metal frames are a distinguishing feature of this skyscraper. They also serve the function of capturing more light.

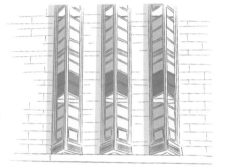

Concrete frame (below)

Unlike many modern skyscrapers, the Mutual Building was constructed of reinforced concrete instead of a steel frame. The exterior is clad in granite with decorative detailing depicting African wildlife and local tribes in a Modernist style, and it features the world's longest (386 feet) carved frieze.

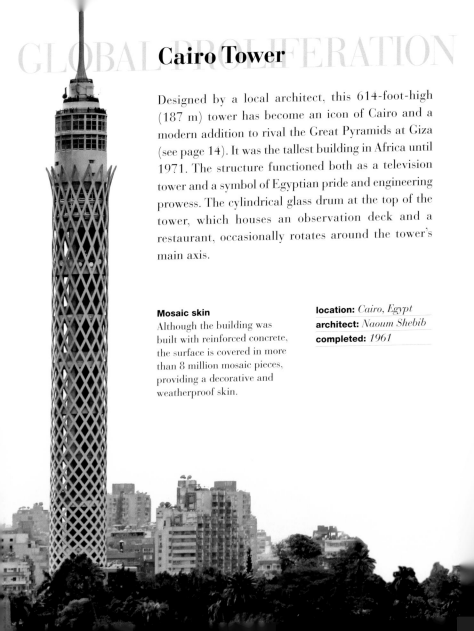

Cairo Tower

Designed by a local architect, this 614-foot-high (187 m) tower has become an icon of Cairo and a modern addition to rival the Great Pyramids at Giza (see page 14). It was the tallest building in Africa until 1971. The structure functioned both as a television tower and a symbol of Egyptian pride and engineering prowess. The cylindrical glass drum at the top of the tower, which houses an observation deck and a restaurant, occasionally rotates around the tower's main axis.

Mosaic skin
Although the building was built with reinforced concrete, the surface is covered in more than 8 million mosaic pieces, providing a decorative and weatherproof skin.

location: *Cairo, Egypt*
architect: *Naoum Shebib*
completed: *1961*

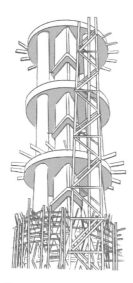

Material symbolism

The staircase and the podium on which the tower stands are lined in polished pink granite from the southern city of Aswan. This material was used extensively by builders in ancient Egypt.

Symbolic structure (above)

The structure stands on a concrete slab that is rooted to the bedrock, 82 feet (25 m) below ground. Above ground, it comprises a reinforced concrete core that houses three elevators and emergency staircases. Four structural columns are attached to the core by circular plates at various intervals and support the exterior lattice frame. The building's diameter is 46 feet (14 m).

Cultural symbolism

The distinctive diamond-shape latticework that wraps around the building's exterior elongates as the tower rises to accentuate the sense of elevation. It opens out at the top to symbolize the lotus flower, which was highly revered in ancient Egypt.

Hôtel Ivoire

The Hôtel Ivoire, dominated by its 25-story tower, was the most conspicuous architectural landmark in Abidjan, the economic capital of post-independence Ivory Coast (Côte d'Ivoire). Commissioned by the state under the leadership of the country's first president, Félix Houphouët-Boigny, the hotel was designed in three phases by two Israeli architects, Heinz Fenchel and Thomas Leitersdorf, with the assistance of the renowned American architect William Pereira and the Israeli developer, Moshe Mayer. The skyscraper was designed to be the centerpiece in a 40-mile-long (64 km) leisure development, dubbed the "African Riviera," promoted by Mayer and intended to be plugged into the global tourist route, housing tens of thousands of locals and attracting hundreds of thousands of hotel guests, but the project ultimately failed.

Military stronghold

From its glamorous origins in the 1970s, the hotel fell from grace during the civil war in the 2000s, when it was used as an impromptu base by soldiers of a French UN peacekeeping mission, whose snipers opened fire on—and killed—several civilian protestors. It has since been completely restored as a hotel.

location: *Abidjan, Ivory Coast*

architects: *Heinz Fenchel, Thomas Leitersdorf, William Pereira, and Moshe Mayer*

completed: *1970*

Neighboring inspiration (left)

The luxurious Hôtel Ivoire exemplified the desire among young African nations (or, more accurately, their leaders) in the postcolonial era to be seen to be part of a sophisticated international elite. It is said that the hotel was commissioned by the president because of his admiration for the Ducor Intercontinental in the capital of neighboring Liberia, Monrovia—a hotel that has since fallen into complete disrepair.

Luxury complex (right)

The hotel comprised a vast landscaped complex with an 80,730-square-foot (7,500 m²) swimming pool and an ice rink. A two-story podium containing a lobby and restaurant supported a 13-story tower (seen far right) with 200 rooms; then, in the late 1960s, the 25-story tower was constructed, adding another 200 rooms.

Palais des Congrès (left)

A white-tiled conference center was added during a third stage of construction in the plaza sited at the foot of the taller tower.

FINDECO House

location: *Lusaka, Zambia*

architects: *Dušan Milenković and Branimir Ganovic*

completed: *1977*

Conceived in 1971 and completed within six years, the 23-story, 296-foot-tall (90 m) headquarters for the Financial and Development Corporation (FINDECO) was designed by two Yugoslavian architects. It was, and remains, Zambia's tallest building, although it was completed just as the country fell into a prolonged depression. Having been occupied by a vast range of different tenants over its lifetime, it has fallen into disrepair in recent years. The huge brutalist structure consists of a massive 18-story block ascending from a three-story concrete podium and cantilevered from a centered core.

Neoclassical elements
The austerity of the building's Modernist appearance, defined by repetitive horizontal bands of concrete and glass, belies the Neoclassical arrangement of its basic elements, which comprise a base (podium), middle (body), and top. Ionized aluminum panels give the main body a greenish-gold appearance.

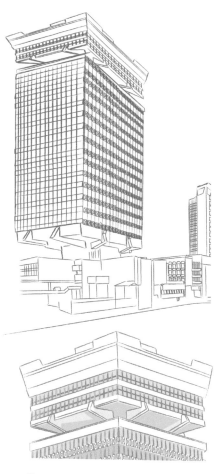

White elephants (left)

Such iconic and relatively expensive structures were invariably commissioned for their symbolism. There was little need to build tall in relatively low-density African cities. Declining economic fortunes caused by the oil crisis in the 1970s led many of these costly buildings to become economically unviable. They now stand as white elephants—redundant monuments to a bygone age of economic and political optimism and independence.

Technological solutions

FINDECO House marks an important transition in the design of high-rises in Africa during the post-independence era. The comparatively plain facade and absence of sun-shading louvers reveal the adoption of technical rather than natural solutions to climatic conditions. Such buildings marked the end of the environmentally responsive "Tropical Modernism" of the 1950s and 1960s and the arrival of Postmodernist architecture.

Concrete crown

A wide beveled band of concrete crowns the top three floors, which are separated from the main body of the building and cantilevered from the core.

Kenyatta International Conference Centre

location: *Nairobi, Kenya*

architects: *David Mutiso and Karl Henrik Nøstvik*

completed: *1973*

Few towers more powerfully evoked the spirit of African independence than Kenya's 32-story Kenyatta International Conference Centre (KICC), designed by a local architect in partnership with a Norwegian. The concrete complex was originally designed to be the headquarters of the Kenya African National Union political party, but during the design process the decision was made to redirect its purpose to house an upcoming World Bank and International Monetary Fund meeting. It then became a catalyst for Kenya's growing prominence as a leading player in Africa.

Growing plans

Mutiso and Nøstvik originally designed a relatively modest 12-story tower, but when it was announced that the complex was to host the 1973 World Bank and IMF meeting, the design was amended and the height of the skyscraper was almost tripled. It was provided with world-class conference facilities and offices that now house the United Nations Environment Programme and UN-Habitat.

Brutalist landmark (left)

The 16-sided, 345-foot (105-m) skyscraper makes a bold architectural statement, but this is accentuated by its raw concrete finish and distinctive *brises-soleil*, which shield the windows to deflect the intense sunlight.

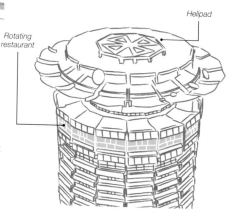

Rotating restaurant

Helipad

Helipad (right)

The skyscraper was crowned with a rotating restaurant affording views of Mount Kenya and Mount Kilimanjaro and, above that, a helipad. The KICC remained the tallest building in Kenya until the 38-story Times Tower was built in Nairobi in 2000.

Amphitheater

At the base of the tower is the distinctive conical form of the main assembly hall, based on the form of a flower with its petals about to unfold. Light enters the amphitheater through a centered skylight.

Nabemba Tower

location: *Brazzaville, Republic of the Congo*
architect: *Jean-Marie Legrand*
completed: *1986*

Designed by the French architect Jean-Marie Legrand, this slender, 348-foot (106-m), 30-story cylinder stands on the banks of the Congo River and dominates the skyline of Brazzaville. The original construction of the office building was funded by the French oil giant Elf and named after the country's tallest mountain, Mont Nabemba. It continues to be a source of local pride, although today's occupants are restricted to various international agencies able to afford the high rents and costly maintenance.

Costly symbol

Severely damaged in the country's civil war in 1997, the building required extensive repairs costing many millions of dollars—more than its original construction. The annual running costs are now in excess of $3 million.

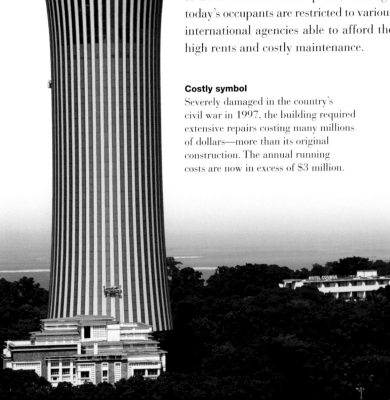

Rival icons

Like many skyscrapers, the building's form was designed to provide a distinctive profile in the city's skyline. Brazzaville also faces old colonial rival Kinshasa (capital of the Democratic Republic of Congo), just across the river, with its own monument in the form of the 656-foot (200-m) Tower of Limete (built in 1971).

Structural core

Rising from a four-story podium, the tower section is suspended from a reinforced concrete core that contains the elevators, emergency stairs, and utilities. Each floor is circular in plan, with the offices occupying the outer section—nearest the windows and natural light. A corridor for circulation encircles the centered core and separates it from the office area.

Streamlined facade

Regular vertical bands of exposed concrete and sealed windows that use reflective glass extend the full height of the tower—a plain exterior that was facilitated by the advent of modern air-conditioning. This eliminated the passive shading that once adorned the facades of high-rise buildings in the tropics.

AWA Building & Tower

location: *Sydney, Australia*

architects: *Robertson, Marks & McCredie / Morrow & Gordon*

completed: *1939*

Although not strictly a skyscraper, the AWA Tower combines the structural functionalism of a communications mast with the early attempts at high-rise construction in the context of Oceania. The tower was designed by Morrow & Gordon to stand on top of a 15-story, steel-frame building designed by Robertson, Marks & McCredie. Completed in 1939, the AWA Tower remained the tallest building in Sydney until 1962, when the AMP building was built. The tower itself was demolished but then rebuilt in 1994, and the entire building is now a protected national heritage asset.

Inspired by Eiffel

The strong and distinctive geometry of the tower's steel frame was inspired by the Eiffel Tower in Paris (see page 40) and the Funkturm Tower in Berlin, completed in 1926.

Amalgamated Wireless Australasia (right)

Until 2000, the building was the headquarters of AWA—a broadcaster, manufacturer of wireless radios, and the first Australian company to manufacture televisions. A sculpted relief of the mythical winged horse Pegasus adorns the top of the brick facade, symbolizing communication.

Art Deco interior (left)

The first-floor interior is lined with silver ash paneling. Above it are plaster reliefs depicting the four elements (air is shown here, center), the signs of the zodiac (left), and symbols of the nations of the world connected through radio (right).

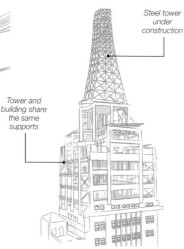

Steel tower under construction

Tower and building share the same supports

Two-part structure

The steel tower stands on the shoulders of a brick-clad, steel-frame building. It was designed as an integral part of the lower half (its supports are part of the structure of the building). The current tower achieves an overall height of 364 feet (111 m) above street level.

MLC Centre

location: *Sydney, Australia*
architect: *Harry Seidler*
completed: *1977*

Trick of the eye
The eight load-bearing columns that surround the building taper slightly until they become flush with the facade at the top of the tower, heightening the effect of the tower rising skyward.

The MLC Centre marks the birth of the modern skyscraper in Australia. Upon completion, at 801 feet (244 m), the complex's 67-story tower became the second tallest reinforced concrete building in the world. The complex comprises a podium at street level, with an outdoor plaza and shopping center, and an octagonal office tower rising at one end around a centered core, with load-bearing concrete columns at each of the eight corners. The octagonal design allowed for a floor plan that was larger and more efficient than a conventional rectilinear plan. The plan also increased wind resistance, allowing for the structure to be made both lighter and cheaper.

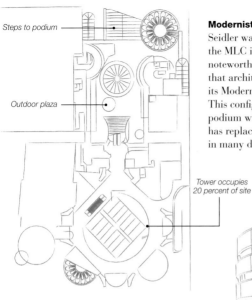

Steps to podium

Outdoor plaza

Tower occupies
20 percent of site

Modernist design

Seidler was a Modernist architect and
the MLC is one of his signature buildings,
noteworthy not just as an example of
that architectural style but also for
its Modernist approach to planning.
This configuration of skyscraper and
podium within a pedestrianized plaza
has replaced the traditional street pattern
in many downtown districts worldwide.

Solar shading (below)

The tower's deeply recessed windows help
reduce solar and heat gain, shading the
interiors and passively reducing the energy
required to cool the building.

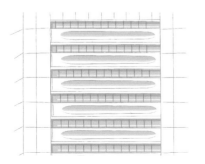

Precast concrete (above)

Modern construction techniques helped
reinforced concrete buildings to rise
taller, faster, and more cheaply, using a
combination of poured concrete and precast
components assembled on site. The various
forms of the complex are unified by their
stark white, exposed concrete finish.

Introduction

Chicago Modernism
German emigrant
architect Ludwig Mies
van der Rohe perfected
a style of Modernist
architecture that
defined corporate
America for decades.
The first crystallization
of his approach to
skyscraper design came
in Chicago in 1949–51,
with the completion of
two 26-story steel and
glass apartment blocks
known as 860–880 Lake
Shore Drive.

The United States dominated the records for the world's
tallest buildings from the 1880s to the 1940s, with
homegrown architects in Chicago and New York
innovating in the Commercial School, neo-Classical,
neo-Gothic, and Art Deco modes. In the 1940s a stream
of Europe's best and brightest architects emigrated to
the country, fleeing persecution and distress in mainland
Europe. They brought new ideas and ideals for an
"International Modernism"—timely for the skyscraper.

World War II proved a transformative moment for
the country. The postwar settlement established a new
world order, in which the culture of U.S. corporate
management, industrial power, and liberal values
would come to dominate the politics and economics of

at least half the globe. A new, corporate image of glass and steel would signal this twentieth-century modernity, reaching increasingly greater heights.

By the mid-1970s the dominance of the corporate image began to fade. Architects sought new solutions to old problems and learned from international rivals. Paradoxically, they turned to older languages of architecture, Classical and Gothic, and gestured toward a playfulness and wit unseen in the sober Modernist establishment in the 1950s and 60s. Postmodernism had its fun, but by the end of the 1990s, it reached an impasse. In the new millennium, skylines of America's great cities were soon punctuated by new, structurally and formally innovative skyscrapers of unprecedented scale.

New York Postmodern
Proponents of Postmodernism had chipped away at Modernism's authority for years before Philip Johnson's AT&T Building in New York City was completed in the mid-1980s. But nothing shattered the confidence of Modernism more than its erstwhile champion, Johnson, slapping a broken pediment on the crown of his tower.

United Nations Building

location: *New York, USA*

architects: *Le Corbusier and Oscar Niemeyer*

completed: *1952*

Green giant

The UN Headquarters consists of four main buildings; its centerpiece the Secretariat at 505 feet (154 m) and 39 stories tall. The design was by a team of international Modernists, chaired by Wallace Harrison of Harrison & Abramovitz.

As World War II came to an end, a new international organization was proposed to replace the failed League of Nations. The United Nations (UN) was established in 1945 to prevent international conflict and to promote justice, respect for the rule of law, and prosperity for all. Initially, the UN harbored dreams of an international city as its headquarters. In the end, this vision had to be scaled back. Nelson Rockefeller's offer of industrial land in Manhattan by the East River was enough to confirm New York as the city of choice for the construction of the UN's permanent home. Establishing an international zone in New York, the UN headquarters have been based there since completion of the buildings in 1952.

Dramatic elevations (left)

Much of the drama of the UN Secretariat Building results from the dramatic profiling of the tower. The north and south elevations are extremely narrow (72 feet/22 m) while the east and west elevations are broad (287 feet/87 m). A similar contrast is produced through glazing—the windowless north and south are faced with Vermont marble, whereas the east and west elevations are entirely glazed in green tinted glass.

Modernism restored (right)

Extensive renovation work began in 2010, repairing leaks, fixing staining, and replacing dangerous materials, such as asbestos paneling. The building had never been closed and had exceeded its expected lifetime by 35 years. All of its 5,040 glazed panes needed replacing. Renovation has restored the glistening, transparent Modernism to the facade.

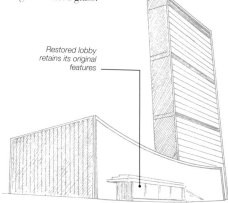

Restored lobby retains its original features

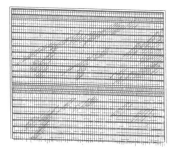

Glass curtain (left)

The Secretariat Building is the first "curtain wall" skyscraper in New York. In earlier skyscrapers, the outer walls were rigid, even if nonloadbearing. A true curtain wall is suspended from the structural frame, attached at the columns or beams. The Secretariat Building's curtain wall consists of aluminum mullions and glass panels, creating a smooth, transparent surface.

Seagram Building

location: *New York, USA*

architects: *Ludwig Mies van der Rohe and Philip Johnson*

completed: *1958*

In June 1954, Samuel Bronfman, CEO of Canadian firm Joseph E. Seagram and Sons (at the time the largest distiller in the world) had plans to build new headquarters for the company in New York. He wrote to his daughter, Phyllis Lambert, then in Paris, about his vision for "Renaissance modernized" and included details of his chosen architect. Lambert wrote back: "NO" and, on returning from Paris, set about approving an architect and developing her own vision, one that would change the face of New York's landscape. In 1958, the Seagram Building was opened, possibly the most sophisticated and elegant (certainly the most expensive) skyscraper yet seen.

Exterior

Phyllis Lambert's selection of Ludwig Mies van der Rohe as the lead architect was inspired. With Le Corbusier, Mies was a prominent and influential proponent of the modern International Style. He had long sought to design a transparent skyscraper and had begun developing his signature style in Chicago at Lake Shore Drive (see page 152). The 38-story Seagram Building was the most striking realization of what he termed "skin-and-bones" architecture.

Minimalist monument

Lambert argued in support of Mies's proposal to set back the entire building, creating an "urban oasis" with its plaza. This freed the design from any zoning regulations and provided a public environment in the center of the city. The organization of the interior and exterior of the building is continuous. The granite used for the plaza extends seamlessly into the building; Mies conceived the curtain wall literally as a "curtain" dividing an open space.

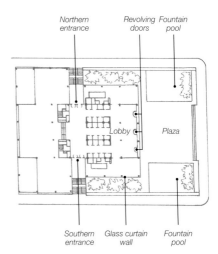

Northern entrance
Revolving doors
Fountain pool
Lobby
Plaza
Southern entrance
Glass curtain wall
Fountain pool

Ordered decoration

Mies strongly approved of the expression of structure in architecture. However, building regulations demanded that steel-and-concrete frames be covered for fire safety. Mies applied continuous bronze-tone I-beams vertically across the entire surface of the Seagram—expressing the underlying structure and reinforcing its spatial qualities.

Lobby

Instead of applying decorative finishes— for example, paint or stucco—to his buildings, Mies, with the assistance of Philip Johnson, used painstaking detailing to expose raw materials. These were carefully chosen and included marble, bronze, steel, glass, leather, and velvet. With the appropriate lighting, this produced a luxurious but refined, corporate atmosphere.

Lever House

location: *New York, USA*

architect: *Skidmore, Owings & Merrill*

completed: *1952*

Completed in 1952, Lever House appears to most as an ordinary office building. Yet it is precisely its unassuming, typical appearance that makes it one of the most important skyscrapers of the twentieth century. Designed by Gordon Bunshaft and Natalie de Blois of Skidmore, Owings & Merrill (SOM), Lever House presented all the features that would dominate corporate American skyscraper design for the next quarter century. SOM would subsequently become one of the largest architectural practices in the world, dominating skyscraper commissions right up to the present day.

Watershed building

Lever House set the standard for curtain-wall skyscraper construction. A strictly flat surface, the cool green tint is produced by the double-glaze, heat-resistant glass. This surface is further articulated by the stainless steel mullions that hold the glass sheets. The concrete frame building allows for open-plan or enclosed offices inside.

No setbacks

Lever House stands 307 feet (94 m) and 24 stories tall. To avoid the setbacks demanded by New York zoning, Bunshaft developed a design of two intersecting blocks—a two-story horizontal slab, with courtyard, taking up the entire plot, and a vertical 21-story slab at its north. Because the vertical slab used only 25 percent of the total site, it was not subject to zoning restrictions.

Clean sweep (below)

By the turn of the century, the original Lever Building was falling into disrepair. A major restoration job was conducted between 1998 and 2001, replacing all of the glass panels with PPG Solex glass, replacing or repairing warped and weathered steel mullions, and introducing concealed aluminum glazing channels. On completion, Lever Building was restored to its crisp, clean original finish.

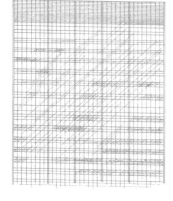

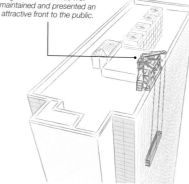

The innovative motor-driven gondola ensured that the glazed facade was well maintained and presented an attractive front to the public.

Advertising to the world

At the-then considerable cost of $50,000, a rooftop gondola was installed to keep the glazing clean. Every six days, it would work across the surface, using "Surf soap," the company's largest selling branded product. Conceived as a means to advertise a Lever product, the gondola subsequently became a standard feature of glass curtain-wall skyscrapers around the world.

Marina City

location: *Chicago, USA*
architect: *Bertrand Goldberg*
completed: *1967*

During the period following World War II, American cities experienced an expansion of residential suburbs at the cost of the inner city. Many architects, who appreciated the cultural and civic benefits of the uptown district sought support for revitalizing the inner urban core. Chicagoan Bertrand Goldberg was one such architect, and with the financial support of the Building Service Employees International Union, he designed one of the most striking additions to the Chicago skyline—Marina City, on the north bank of Chicago River. His "city within a city" was intended to reinvigorate the city center and reverse the flight to the suburbs.

The city within a city

Goldberg began designing Marina City in 1959 and construction was complete by 1967. A complex of five buildings, Marina City includes retail space, a theater, parking facilities, offices, and residential units, and it occupies an entire block in the city's Loop district. The most striking feature of the complex is its twin residential towers—at 587 feet (179 m) and 65 stories—which, at the time of their completion, were the world's tallest residential buildings.

"Pie-shape" living (right)

The residential towers were originally built as apartments, with 16 per floor, but they are now individually owned condominiums. Arranged in sections, so that each unit culminates in an extravagently curved balcony, Goldberg's design gave every occupant access to outside space.

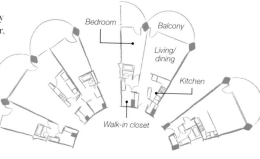

Bedroom

Balcony

Living/dining

Kitchen

Walk-in closet

Everything under one roof (left)

The elevator core at the center of each tower houses five elevators and is surrounded by a circular hallway, which provides access to apartments from the 21st to the 60th floors. The first 19 floors are exposed spiral parking ramps, with a total of around 896 parking spaces. On the 20th floor of each tower are laundry services, storage, and a small gym. Atop each building are 360-degree viewing decks.

Organic form (right)

The circular plan and overall design of Marina City is deliberately at odds with the dominant style of "corporate America" of the postwar period. Rejecting Mies van der Rohe's and SOM's reduced, modular Modernism, Goldberg embraced the Expressionist mode—using reinforced concrete to create humanistic, sculptural forms. His two towers were quickly dubbed the "corncob" condominiums.

John Hancock Center/ 875 North Michigan Avenue

location: *Chicago, USA*

architect: *Skidmore, Owings & Merrill*

completed: *1968*

Chicago boasts another kind of high-rise Expressionist architecture—this time structural rather than formal. When the John Hancock Center (now called 875 North Michigan Avenue) topped out in 1968, a new form of skyscraper structure was introduced: the "trussed tubular system." Pioneered by Fazlur Khan of SOM, the building stood at 1,127 feet (344 m) tall and encompassed 100 stories of open-plan offices, restaurants, and 700 condominiums. On completion, the world's second tallest building became iconic. It has featured in many movies and often been referenced in popular culture.

Tubular structure

The original engineering wasn't by any means all perfect. Initial calculations for the loading of the foundations were significantly short of requirements—work was halted after the construction of only 20 stories, due to subsidence. The long delays and an $11 million repair bill resulted in bankruptcy for the lead developer, Jerry Wolman.

Open plan (right)

While the crossbracing on the exterior does restrict some of the views from the building, it affords significant amounts of space within. Because the interior columns are only required to support dead loads (instead of significant wind loads and earth movement forces), the design team was able to provide large open spaces for the mixed-use tower.

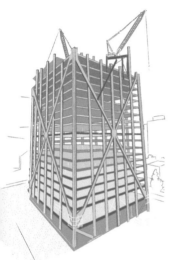

The X factor

Gigantic X braces, combined with the strong columns and beams on the exterior of the building, are part of the tubular system developed by structural engineer Fazlur Khan. It creates a hollow tube structure that can resist lateral loads (such as strong winds or earthquakes), preventing the building from toppling and allowing for the interior to be freed of columns.

Pool with a view

Iconic in the landscape of Chicago, "big John," as it is locally known, has a SkyWalk observatory on the 94th floor, a swimming pool with panoramic views on the 44th floor, and numerous restaurants make the tower a top attraction as well as a constant visual presence.

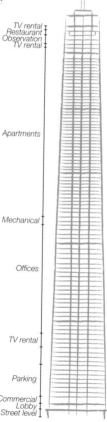

TV rental
Restaurant
Observation
TV rental

Apartments

Mechanical

Offices

TV rental

Parking

Commercial
Lobby
Street level

World Trade Center

location: *New York, USA*

architect: *Minoru Yamasaki*

completed: *1973*

Twin Towers

Until September 11, 2001, the World Trade Center was the tallest building in New York City, of which the North Tower (or One World Trade Center) was the taller of the two towers, by 6 feet (1.8 m), distinguishable by its communications mast (adding a further 360 feet/110 m). Otherwise the towers were identical. The public could gain access to the sky lobby in the South Tower, and this platform allowed views of up to 50 miles (80 km).

Although the "Twin Towers" of the World Trade Center in New York will be indelibly associated with the dreadful events of 9/11, it is worth recalling their architecture and engineering, as the pinnacle of corporate American skyscraper design of the mid-twentieth century. Completed in 1973 as part of the Lower Manhattan urban renewal project spearheaded by the banker and philanthropist David Rockefeller, the building combined the most advanced structural technology with the unique sensibilities of American architect Minoru Yamasaki.

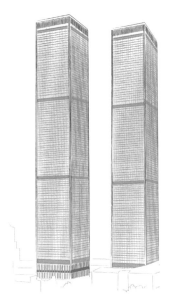

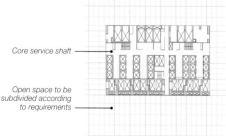

Core service shaft

Open space to be
subdivided according
to requirements

Flexible interior (above)

By using the tube frame structure,
Yamasaki completely freed the floor
space of the towers, maximizing the
yield of usable space throughout.
The core service shaft—housing
elevators, stairwells, washrooms,
air-conditioning, energy supplies,
and telecommunications—measured
87 by 137 feet (27 by 42 m). It was
surrounded by open space that could
be subdivided as required, and all
was encased in a 208-square-foot
(19-m²) envelope of steel,
aluminum-alloy, and glass.

Tube frame (above)

Yamasaki utilized the tube frame
structure engineering principle—
an exterior frame resists lateral
loads, and, in this instance,
supports the internal floors. Each
facade consisted of fifty-nine
17-inch (43-cm) columns on a
40-inch (102-cm) grid. Each set
of three columns combined into
one at the lobby on the first floor.
This had two effects. First, all
windows were narrow and tall—
a benefit, in Yamasaki's view, who
had a fear of heights. Second, the
tower facades appeared extremely
"flat," like taut textiles.

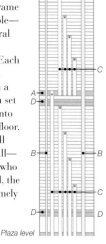

Plaza level

Elevator efficiency (left)

At 110 stories, the towers required a
complex of elevators to service each
story efficiently. The towers were
divided into thirds, and two "sky
lobbies"(A) inserted. These were
serviced by express elevators (B)
and allowed for users to access local
elevator services (C). Mechanical
plant decks (D) were also inserted.

Sears Tower/Willis Tower

location: *Chicago, USA*

architect: *Skidmore, Owings & Merrill*

completed: *1973*

Bundled tube structure
The Willis Tower has a highly distinctive form. It was designed by the SOM team behind the John Hancock Center. Developed by Fazlur Khan, the tower is, in fact, a "bundle" of nine square tubes in a three-by-three configuration. This bundle is contained on a 225-foot (69-m) base and provides impressive structural efficiencies.

At 110 stories and 1,450 feet (442 m), the Sears Tower (now renamed Willis) in Chicago was the tallest building in the world on completion in 1973. It remains the second tallest building in the western hemisphere (after completion in 2013 of One World Trade Center, see page 228). Originally commissioned by the retailer Sears, Roebuck & Co., naming rights of the building were granted to the Willis Group (a financial group) that took up office space in 2009. The building remains one of Chicago's largest tourist attractions in terms of visitor numbers, and many Chicagoans continue to refer to it as the Sears Tower.

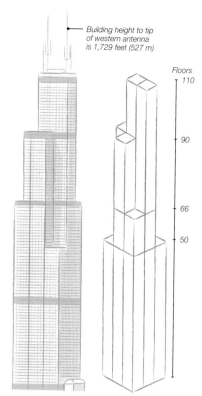

Building height to tip of western antenna is 1,729 feet (527 m)

Floors
110

90

66

50

Tubular frame (left)

Each of the nine towers is itself a tubular frame structure. These support one another in turn. The tubes are staggered in height: the northwest and southeast tubes end at the 50th floor; the northeast and southwest tubes end at the 66th floor; the north, east and south tubes end at the 90th floor; the remaining center and west tubes rise to its full height of 110 floors.

Black belts (above left)

The facade of the tower is further broken up by four deep bands: at the 29th–32nd floors, the 64th–65th floor, the 88th–89th floors, and the 104th–108th floors. These bands, which are picked out in black on the facade, conceal "truss belts" that provide further lateral support and louvered ventilation for services.

Skydeck balconies

Huge numbers of tourists are attracted to the Willis Tower and its "Skydeck." Located on the 103rd floor, the observation deck provides spectacular views of Chicago and the Midwest. Higher than any other observation deck in the country, since 2009, visitors can experience the added thrill of standing on retractable glass balconies.

AT&T Building/
550 Madison Avenue

location: *New York, USA*
architects: *Philip Johnson and John Burgee*
completed: *1984*

Postmodern pediment
Philip Johnson had done more to champion Modernism than any other architect in the world. He co-curated the "International Style" exhibition at the Museum of Modern Art in New York in 1932 and contributed to the Seagram Building design by Mies van der Rohe in 1958. But in 1979 the intellectually restless, self-styled avant-gardist Johnson announced the end of Modernism, with his strangely detailed skyscraper.

In 1984, New York managed to beat the world at a new game for skyscrapers. The AT&T Building, as it was then called, was not the tallest, nor the most technologically advanced building in the world, but it was the "wittiest" and, more than any other building, it smashed the dogma of the modern International Style. Designed by Philip Johnson and John Burgee, the building, capped by a broken pediment typical on the top of eighteenth-century English case furniture, announced the end of Modernism and the supremacy of Postmodernism.

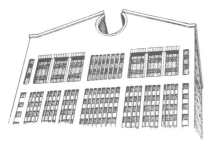

Broken pediment (left)

The building's standout feature is its broken-pedimented top, a classical motif applied to a modern skyscraper. The 647-foot (197-m), 37-story building relies on a typical steel load-bearing frame structure, but it is faced in Connecticut granite panels.

Grand entrance (below)

If the top of 550 Madison Avenue is its most well-known feature, the giant entrance lobby at its base is most remarkable. The plan is narrow, but at seven stories high, the arch and columns reference Romanesque architecture. Within, the barrel vault loggia, which formerly housed an oversize statue of "The Genius of Electricity" (by Evelyn Beatrice Longman, and taken from the roof of the original AT&T building), produces an extraordinary effect.

Grand exit (above)

Throughout the building, Johnson and Burgee added classical details. Instead of adhering to a particular style or period, the designers willfully mixed strict classical with baroque elements. The staircases, encased in white marble with black veins, are one such example.

PPG Place

location: *Pittsburgh, USA*

architects: *Philip Johnson and John Burgee*

completed: *1984*

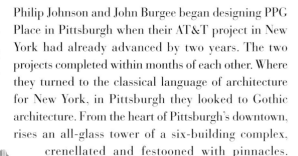

Philip Johnson and John Burgee began designing PPG Place in Pittsburgh when their AT&T project in New York had already advanced by two years. The two projects completed within months of each other. Where they turned to the classical language of architecture for New York, in Pittsburgh they looked to Gothic architecture. From the heart of Pittsburgh's downtown, rises an all-glass tower of a six-building complex, crenellated and festooned with pinnacles. It reflects light and the Pittsburgh skyline in celebration of the principal manufacturing product of the anchor tenant, PPG (formerly Pittsburgh Plate Glass Company).

Gothic glass

Johnson and Burgee differ in their use of the Gothic from the skyscraper pioneers of the 1920s because they produce a diagrammatic outline, not a completely realized Gothic facade. The qualities of the cladding material, mirrored glass, are respected and enhanced by presenting multifaceted facades that reflect light and shadows. Mirrored double-glazing also provides significant environmental gains (reflecting heat in the summer, and retaining infrared warmth in the winter).

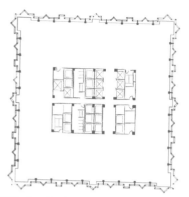

Pleated perimeter (above)

The glass curtain wall of PPG Place produces a pleating effect on the surface through the introduction of false piers. These alternate between square and diamond forms, further breaking up the surface. End piers accentuate the folding of the surface. A million square feet of PPG Solarban 550 reflective glass was used, with 175 unique extrusions to produce this pleating effect.

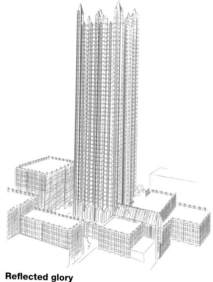

Reflected glory

The main tower stands at 635 feet (194 m) and 40 stories. It is surrounded by a mixed complex—another tower of 14 stories and four six-story buildings that integrate the tower into the wider urban fabric. Together, they produce an enclosed plaza, recalling the great public squares of European cities.

Winter garden

Two other types of glass are used in the complex. Clear double glazing encloses the 13,000-square-foot (1,200-m²) winter garden, which is filled with plants and bathed in light and warmth. The garden is open to the public daily and is also used as a performance and event venue. The shopping arcades are also clear glazed. Elsewhere, between each floor, and at all mechanical plant areas, a type of spandrel glass is backed with fiberglass.

Humana Building

location: *Louisville, Kentucky*

architect: *Michael Graves*

completed: *1985*

Taking a different approach from Johnson and Burgee, Michael Graves was another American architect who broke with Modernist convention. Instead of relying on historical references to imbue his architecture with visual power, Graves used basic geometric shapes and flat surfaces to produce complex and imaginative buildings. His design for the headquarters of the Humana Corporation in Louisville, Kentucky, displays the playfulness of his approach to architecture. Standing 417 feet (127 m), with 26 stories, the Humana tower has four entirely different facades and a sloping pyramid top, a distinctive form that locally earned it the nickname "milk carton."

Postmodern pink

Graves finished the entire building with a pink granite cladding. The tower is capped with a triangular pyramid form, distinctive from miles around. But for these two features, every aspect of each facade is different. Graves argued that his skyscraper design responded to the unique aspects of each side of the building plot.

North facade (below)

The north facade provides the clearest expression of a tripartite division of the building. The eight-story base includes an enormous loggia, capped with a narrow triangular glass pediment. The main shaft of the tower is set deep back from the front of the loggia and rises a further 12 stories, with small symmetrical square openings. The top is marked with a large glazed surface, punctuated by a metal truss, upon which rests a curved protrusion. The whole is capped with a sloping pyramid.

The truss work replicates the steel bridges crossing the Ohio River, many of which are visible from this vantage point

South facade (above)

The south facade is different from the north. It too is organized as a tripartite division, but maintains a sheer face, continuous from base to cap. The stronger division is vertical, with a central three-bay curved surface running from the eighth floor to the top. Although various elements reflect the north face, the south facade reads as a completely different building.

Geometrical inlays

Graves clad the exterior of the Humana Building in pink granite, but the interior is faced with a panoply of colored marbles and metal inlays. Again, unlike Johnson and Burgee, Graves developed his own architectural language, instead of referring to classical architecture, although it retained a strong geometrical expression.

173

Norwest Center/ Wells Fargo Center

While many consider the architecture of César Pelli in the same Postmodern category as other architects of the 1980s, Pelli describes himself as a Modernist. Regardless of how his designs might be categorized, it is clear that one of his breakthrough buildings, the Wells Fargo Center (formerly the Norwest Center) in Minneapolis, recalls the Art Deco of the past and works visually with the urban context, while maintaining Modernist values of honesty of structure and truth to materials. Completed in 1988, at 774 feet (236 m), it remains the third tallest building in the city.

location: *Minneapolis, USA*
architect: *César Pelli & Associates*
completed: *1988*

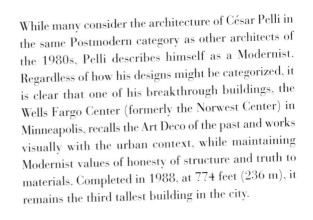

Art Deco leanings
Pelli's design emphasizes the verticality of the 57-story tower of the Wells Fargo Center. First, he reproduced the setback designs of the 1920s and 30s, perfected by Raymond Hood for the RCA Tower of the Rockefeller Center (see page 90) in New York. Second, Pelli introduced geometric detailing of the cladding material. Finally, he specified narrow portrait windows.

Rotunda

The Wells Fargo Center provides a public environment with a rotunda, flanked by two buildings containing boardrooms and office suites. Pelli incorporated fittings and fixtures—such as iron railings—salvaged from the former Norwest Bank headquarters (built in 1930), destroyed by fire in 1982.

Urban setting (right)

The tower itself is part of a larger complex. Norwest Bank requested a design from Pelli covering two city blocks. In the procurement process one block was lost, Pelli adjusted the design, and as a result the building is more sympathetic to the urban site. The Center offers almost 1.5 million gross square feet (139,350 m²) of space.

The energy-efficient building received one of the first Energy Star labels from the U.S. Environmental Protection Agency

Rotunda

Natural stone

The facade of the Norwest Center is largely faced with pink buff Minnesota stone. The qualities of this stone are heightened by contrasting with the white New Imperial granite that Pelli specified for the peaks of the building, and major opening surrounds. Glazing is set back 6 inches (15 cm) deep from the surface.

Scholastic Building/ 557 Broadway

location: *New York, USA*
architects: *Aldo Rossi / Morris Adjmi*
completed: *2001*

The final word in Postmodern skyscraper design, the Scholastic Building, at only ten stories, barely ranks as a skyscraper among today's mega- and hypertall towers. Its designer, the highly regarded Italian architect Aldo Rossi, was enormously influential. Much of his theory of architecture was based on an understanding of classical Italian buildings and urban forms. With the Scholastic, he attempted an application of those theories to the New York context, with particular reference to the nineteenth-century iron-frame facades that identify several commercial buildings in SoHo and Tribeca districts. Rossi died before completion of the building, his work finished by Morris Adjmi.

Kit design

Rossi adopted the "kit-of-parts" approach of late-nineteenth-century builders for whom the cheapness and availability of cast iron prompted the use of precast components. Based on an iron frame, facades were visually enhanced by the purchase and application of kits bought from catalogs. Although customized, the Scholastic's red iron beams, resting on cylindrical piers with recessed green spandrels, appear entirely in keeping with its neighbors.

New kid on the block (left)

The building site is located in the historic "iron-frame" district of SoHo in Manhattan, which has had strong preservation and conservation orders since 1973. When the publishers Scholastic purchased 557 Broadway in the early 1990s, their new building had to conform to the conservation area. Rossi and his New York practice produced a design in 1994 that was passed by the Landmarks Preservation Commission within an hour of deliberation.

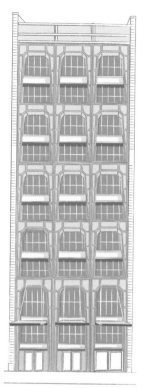

Basement theater

The interior of the Scholastic includes a small basement theater, modeled on one designed by Palladio in Vicenza, northeast Italy, in the sixteenth century. It provided twice the allotted floor space for the Scholastic site. The combination of historical reference and modern design results in a building that satisfied its client and conservationists alike.

Rear facade

The building's Mercer Street facade is as interesting as the one on Broadway. Eschewing the cylindrical columns, the facade relies entirely on the expressive qualities of the bolted, steel structural walls. Flatter, clearly utilitarian, but providing as much, if not more, light to the interior office space, the building responds to the wider industrial urban fabric.

Eight Spruce Street

location: *New York, USA*
architect: *Gehry Partners*
completed: *2011*

A startling reminder of the continuing possibilities for innovation in skyscraper design arrived in New York in 2011. The architect Frank Gehry—internationally famous for his designs of crumpled, fractured, folded titanium facades for art museums across Europe, China, and the Americas—had not been able to gain a foothold in Manhattan or a residential commission in the city. The developer Forest City Ratner provided that opportunity, and between 2006 and 2010 Gehry's 76-story tower rose to 870 feet (265 m), presenting a unique expression of the typical New York skyscraper.

Mixed-use tower

Strict zoning had prevented Forest City Ratner from utilizing a site in the downtown area. However, a trade-off was found between the City planning officers and the developer. The tower at Eight Spruce Street delivers a public elementary school, hospital services, and retail space across the first five floors, expressed with a simple, brick, exterior.

Facade in close up

Gehry's office used 3D modeling software—the same he used for the Guggenheim Bilbao museum in Spain—to generate precise dimensions for each panel. The panels were then manufactured and assembled on-site. Due to the efficiency of the modeling, even though 10,500 individual panels were used, no extra cost was incurred.

Undulating edifice (below)

Gehry's tower is clad in steel panels that appear to ripple or undulate across the otherwise typical stepped, orthogonal skyscraper produced by New York's strict zoning laws. The steel reflects light in such a way that, throughout the day, the surface takes on almost a liquid quality.

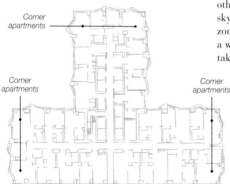

Corner apartments

Corner apartments

Corner apartments

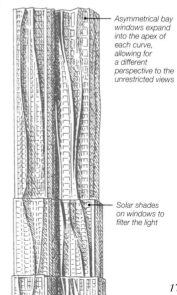

Asymmetrical bay windows expand into the apex of each curve, allowing for a different perspective to the unrestricted views

Solar shades on windows to filter the light

Maximizing views (above)

The T-plan of Eight Spruce Street provides six corner apartments per floor. The building was, on completion, one of the tallest residential structures in the western hemisphere, and, although originally planned as a mix of rental apartments and condominiums, since completion, it provides 903 rental homes.

432 Park Avenue

location: *New York, USA*
architect: *Rafael Viñoly*
completion: *2015*

Dizzy heights

The building provides a startlingly simple profile. The extreme ratio of height to width (15:1, greater than most other towers) and austere regularity of openings (exactly three openings, per floor, per face) creates a highly abstracted quality. Many have criticized the building for this almost mute quality.

The completion of 432 Park Avenue inaugurated a new age in residential skyscrapers for New York. Increased concentration of capital in real estate in Manhattan has encouraged developers to request maximization of height in relation to footprint. Designed by Uruguayan architect Rafael Viñoly, and engineered by WSP New York, in 2015, 432 Park Avenue was, at 1,397 feet (426 m) and 85 floors, the tallest residential tower in the world. Providing 146 condominium apartments, its radical formal simplicity has divided critics and the public alike.

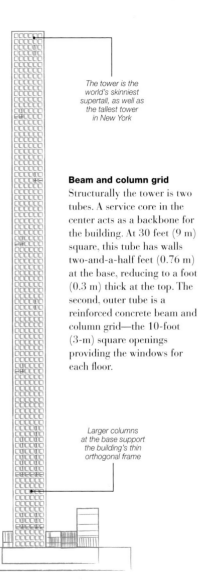

The tower is the world's skinniest supertall, as well as the tallest tower in New York

Beam and column grid

Structurally the tower is two tubes. A service core in the center acts as a backbone for the building. At 30 feet (9 m) square, this tube has walls two-and-a-half feet (0.76 m) at the base, reducing to a foot (0.3 m) thick at the top. The second, outer tube is a reinforced concrete beam and column grid—the 10-foot (3-m) square openings providing the windows for each floor.

Larger columns at the base support the building's thin orthogonal frame

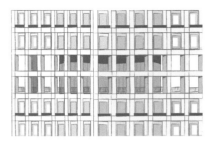

Unglazed openings

At such a high floor-to-height ratio, wind loads can cause unpleasant, even violent, sway. To counter this, each 12th floor is used for mechanical plant (freeing even more space for the apartments). These have no glazing, allowing for wind to flow through the building. A damper on the top floor creates 1,433 tons of counterweight to movement.

Head space

Although the building at 432 Park Avenue is resolutely private, its occupants are also provided with spectacular views outward. The smallest condominiums are studios; the largest is a six-bedroom, seven-bath penthouse with a library.

56 Leonard Street

location: *New York, USA*

architect: *Herzog & de Meuron*

completion: *2016*

Rising above the otherwise low-rise area of Tribeca, New York, stands 56 Leonard Street, popularly referred to as the Jenga tower, after the wooden block game. Designed by Herzog & de Meuron, the tower is 821 feet (250 m) tall and 60 stories high, providing 145 condominiums. However, it is neither the height nor the number of apartments that stands out. The Swiss architects aimed to design a "cluster of country villas" in the sky, and the otherwise simple base ascends into a collection of brilliantly articulated boxes.

Room at the top

Every one of the 146 apartments at 56 Leonard Street has some kind of outdoor space. At the lower levels, this is achieved with cantilevered balconies, puncturing the glazed curtain wall. Higher up, however, entire floor plates cantilever out from the concrete core, until, at the upper ten stories, distinct villas appear to rest unsupported in the sky.

Luxury living (right)

The condominiums are aimed at a luxury market. Ten elevator shafts service the building, and no more than two apartments share the same elevator. Midlevel amenity floors provide a private swimming pool, a gym, screening rooms, and children's play areas. The lobby is lined with black granite, and the public realm at street level is dominated by a giant Anish Kapoor mirrored sculpture.

Raw beauty

The dominant material throughout the building is concrete. This has been left "raw" (*béton brut* in French) in the amenity areas, providing a highly expressive, textured surface, which is offset by rich hardwoods and elegant light fittings.

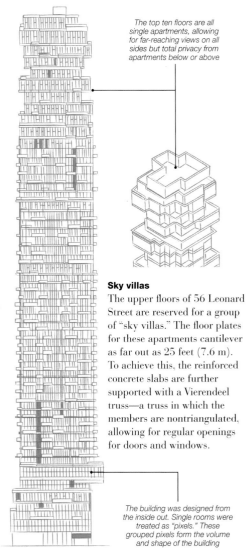

The top ten floors are all single apartments, allowing for far-reaching views on all sides but total privacy from apartments below or above

Sky villas

The upper floors of 56 Leonard Street are reserved for a group of "sky villas." The floor plates for these apartments cantilever as far out as 25 feet (7.6 m). To achieve this, the reinforced concrete slabs are further supported with a Vierendeel truss—a truss in which the members are nontriangulated, allowing for regular openings for doors and windows.

The building was designed from the inside out. Single rooms were treated as "pixels." These grouped pixels form the volume and shape of the building

American Copper Buildings

location: *New York, USA*
architect: *SHoP/JDS*
completion: *2018*

Leaning towers

The complex form of
the towers is a result
of analysis of possible
configurations given the
strict zoning codes. Both
towers "lean" into the
center, maximizing the
height and floorspace
available on the plot of
land. This opens up two
major amenity features:
a street-level park and
through routes, and
a midlevel suite of
spaces at the bridge.

The latest addition to New York's Manhattan skyline
appears, from the distance, like two dancing figures,
the taller of which holds out its arm to catch the other
by the waist as it gently leans back. Designed by SHoP
Architects for JDS Development, the residential towers
are graceful, if peculiar, statements on the possibilities
of structural engineering in concrete and steel today.
The taller West Tower reaches 540 feet (165 m), the
shorter East Tower 470 feet (143 m), providing a total
of 761 rental units.

Trilevel sky bridge (right)

The bridge is one of the more striking features of the towers. Located 300 feet (91 m) above ground, the bridge has three levels and provides amenities for residents in both towers. These include a swimming pool, a lounge, a gym, restaurant and bar, and children's play areas.

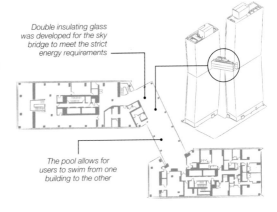

Double insulating glass was developed for the sky bridge to meet the strict energy requirements

The pool allows for users to swim from one building to the other

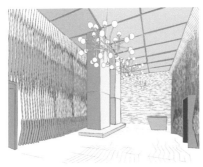

Behind the scenes (left)

As much of the innovation in the design is hidden as revealed. Planned in the aftermath of Hurricane Sandy, a key concern for the developer and architectural team was the impact of climate change and rising sea levels. All aspects of the building design have been made with consideration for possible water damage. The open wood paneling in the lobby is not a purely aesthetic design decision; the panels will dry undamaged in the event of flooding.

Copper cladding

The surface of the towers is as distinctive as their form. Clad entirely in copper on completion, they stand in bright shining metallic hues. However, these will change rapidly, oxidizing and producing a mottling of green, until a deep, matte hue of green covers the building as a whole, reflecting the Statue of Liberty 5 miles (8 km) away in the Upper Bay.

Introduction

Cultivating form
Nishi-Shinjuku is
Tokyo's commercial
heart and home to
12 of the city's tallest
buildings, including the
Mode Gakuen Cocoon
Tower, which houses
three universities. Its
shape is intended to
reference the nurturing
of the students within.

By their very nature, skyscrapers are designed to
attract attention, and architects are paid handsomely
to concoct all manner of weird and wonderful forms,
designed to stand out from the crowd. The result has
been a increasing array of peculiar shapes that, for
better or for worse, have transformed or defined urban
skylines everywhere.

The rise of the unconventional has also been
paralleled by rapid advances in digital technologies,
as well as new materials and construction techniques,
which have enabled mind-boggling advances in

design and engineering, pushing the boundaries of form and height to extremes. Today, computers can calculate every detail of a building, its performance, and its structural integrity long before construction has even begun. From twisted torsos and mammoth elephants to gardens in the sky, the urban landscape is becoming increasingly marked by the quest for distinction, forged through the age-old alliance of affluent clients and imaginative architects, but on an entirely new scale—a trend that looks set to continue well into the twenty-first century.

Nakagin Capsule Tower

This remarkable accumulation of cuboid capsules was among the most influential innovations in residential skyscraper design in the twentieth century. Constructed on the periphery of Tokyo's world-famous Ginza District, this radical 11-story tower was part of a wider social experiment that reconceived urban living. Designed for single male workers, the concept was based on providing accommodation in the form of individual apartment capsules that could be easily replaced and upgraded.

location: *Tokyo, Japan*
architect: *Kisho Kurokawa*
completed: *1972*

Decline and revival

The experiment ultimately proved unsuccessful, because the living standards were deemed very poor, the building's concrete exterior was viewed negatively, maintenance costs rose exponentially, and the capsules proved too costly to replace. With demolition proposed in 2007, a campaign led by the architect, Kurokawa, was launched to save this unique skyscraper.

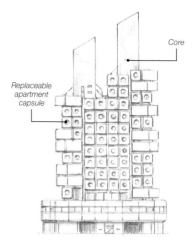

Core

Replaceable apartment capsule

Capsule living (below)

Each capsule comprised a concrete exterior with plastic furnishings inside and a single circular window (3 feet/0.9 cm in diameter) to provide natural light. Each pod measured 7 feet 6 inches by 12 feet by 6 feet 9½ inches (2.3 by 3.7 by 2.1 m) and contained a compact fully-functioning, self-contained apartment with all the latest modern conveniences, including television, music center, refrigerator, and modern bathroom.

Metabolism (above)

The concept became the showpiece of the Metabolist movement, which advocated a new dynamic form of architecture that could adapt to a city's changing landscape over time. The 140 apartment capsules were designed to be replaceable at the end of their life and upgraded.

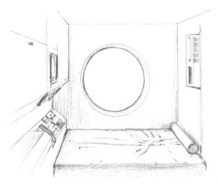

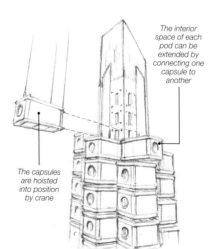

The interior space of each pod can be extended by connecting one capsule to another

The capsules are hoisted into position by crane

Prefabrication

Each capsule was designed and built in a factory and transported to the site on a truck and fixed to the core at the center with four high-tension bolts and simply plugged into services and amenities, such as electricity and water supply.

HSBC Headquarters (Hong Kong)

location: *Hong Kong, China*

architect: *Foster + Partners*

completed: *1985*

In the early 1920s, when the senior architect of Palmer & Turner, George Wilson, was commissioned to design new headquarters for HSBC on Shanghai's riverfront, he was instructed to "spare no expense, but dominate the Bund." The same spirit was evoked a half century later when HSBC commissioned the British architect, Norman Foster, to "create the best bank in the world." When completed in November 1985, the 586-foot (179-m) high new headquarters in Hong Kong was the most expensive building ever constructed, at a cost of US $668 million.

Skeletal structure

The distinctive skeletal structure with its "coat-hanger" trusses visible on the exterior, reveals the innovative architectural and engineering solutions that allow for the floors to be suspended from five pairs of steel masts instead of being supported on a conventional steel frame or reinforced concrete core. Consequently, all services (water, waste, elevators, fire stairs, etc.) are on the building's perimeter.

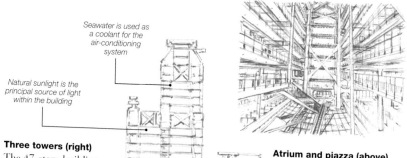

Natural sunlight is the principal source of light within the building

Seawater is used as a coolant for the air-conditioning system

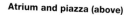

Three towers (right)

The 47-story building actually comprises three interconnected slender towers of 29, 36, and 44 stories above ground, arranged like books on a shelf that give it a staggered profile from the side. Site constraints meant that the massive steel structure had to be manufactured off-site: 33,000 tons of steel components fabricated in Great Britain were shipped to Hong Kong, and assembled on-site.

Atrium and piazza (above)

The absence of a service core allowed the building to be suspended above the ground to create a public piazza at street level beneath a 170-foot (52-m), ten-story atrium that is flooded with natural light "scooped" into the building via giant mirrors in the roof.

The structural steel came from Great Britain, the aluminum cladding, floor, and glass from the United States, and the service modules from Japan

Stephen

Feng shui

The building's design was informed by the principles of feng shui, including the relationship with the sea in front and the mountain behind, and the pair of bronze figures, Stephen and Stitt (former bank managers), guarding the entrance.

Stitt

30 St. Mary Axe

location: *London, UK*

architect: *Foster + Partners*

completed: *2003*

Structural innovation

The distinctive diagrid structure, weighing 2,755 tons, was inspired by the lightweight structural airframe design by the British engineer Barnes Wallis, inventor of the bouncing bomb, and the geodesic structures made famous by the renowned American architect Buckminster Fuller. This structural resolution allows for each floor to twist by 5 degrees, giving the tower its distinctive spiraling skin made up of 5,500 diamond-shape glass panels.

The idiosyncratic 41-story streamlined body of 30 St. Mary Axe, affectionately nicknamed "The Gherkin," has become one of London's most iconic buildings. The 590-foot-tall (180 m) building was conceived to the highest possible environmental standards, with a double outer skin to regulate temperatures and densely planted internal "sky gardens" to cleanse and oxygenate the recycled air within the building and reduce the need for air-conditioning. The compact design comprises a main core containing elevators and services, affording the offices unrestricted views from the windows.

Sky garden (left)

The building's innovative sky gardens were inspired by Foster's previous work with Buckminster Fuller on the Climatroffice (1971) and other precedents that included internal vertical gardens, such as the Willis Faber offices in Ipswich, UK (1975), and the Commerzbank offices in Frankfurt (1997).

Wind resistance (right)

The distinctive barrel-like shape, the widest point of which is on the 16th floor, reduces wind pressure and structural weight, and it improves street-level conditions by eliminating the downdrafts that menace the narrow alleys and medieval street pattern of the City of London.

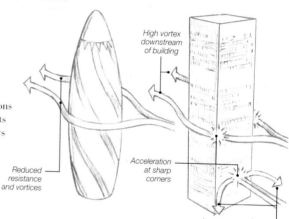

High vortex downstream of building

Reduced resistance and vortices

Acceleration at sharp corners

updraft and downdraft

Meeting the street

Built on the site of the former Baltic Exchange, which was destroyed by an IRA bomb in 1992, the building's relationship with the street is exceptionally well designed, where the elegant form diminishes in width to meet the street as an uninterrupted circle. The absence of service buildings, goods entrances, and other subsidiary structures that so often clutter the bases of skyscrapers allows for the creation of a small public piazza.

Lloyd's Building

Conceived in the late 1970s, the headquarters of the insurance company Lloyd's of London exemplifies the High Tech movement that the architect Richard Rogers helped pioneer. Standing at 312 feet (95 m) tall, the ultramodern building is designed "inside out," with all the services arranged on the outside so that the floorspace within is open plan and flexible and a 249-foot-high (76 m) atrium can occupy the center of the building, flooding it with natural light.

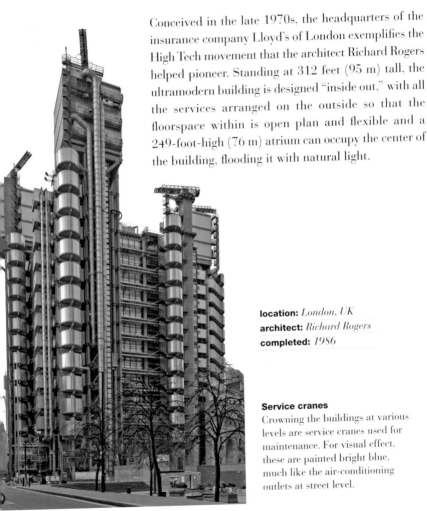

location: *London, UK*
architect: *Richard Rogers*
completed: *1986*

Service cranes

Crowning the buildings at various levels are service cranes used for maintenance. For visual effect, these are painted bright blue, much like the air-conditioning outlets at street level.

Structural innovation (right)

The combined weight of the floors is supported by 28 reinforced concrete columns: six high-grade concrete towers support polished stainless-steel services, such as elevators, fire stairs, water piping, and air-conditioning ducting, all visually expressed on the exterior. The project required more than 43,800 cubic yards (33,510 m³) of concrete and 35,800 square yards (30,000 m²) of stainless steel.

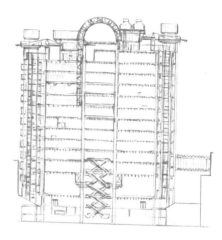

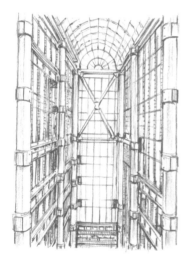

The atrium (left)

The magnificent 14-story atrium dominates the building's interior, with its glass and steel frame visible from the southern elevation paying homage to the adjacent nineteenth-century Leadenhall Market and inspired by Joseph Paxton's Crystal Palace (see page 38).

Georgian gem

The original wood-panel dining room designed by Robert Adam in 1763 was salvaged from the previous Lloyd's office and reassembled in the new high-tech building, where it is used as a board room.

Al Bahr Towers

location: *Abu Dhabi, UAE*

architect: *AHR*

completed: *2012*

One of the greatest challenges for skyscrapers of the future will be their environmental performance. The pioneering and high-tech Al Bahr Towers in Abu Dhabi draws inspiration from the ancient screening system known as mashrabiya. However, what makes these modern mashrabiya so innovative is that they are programmed to open and close in response to the sun's daily trajectory. Each of the triangular units comprises an aluminum frame and a semitransparent PTFE-coated glass-fiber fabric that independently responds to the sun's movement, animating the building and giving it a distinctive and dynamic character.

Supergreen

The dynamic skin covering all but the northern facades of the Al Bahr Towers is made up of 2,098 mashrabiya units that open and close in response to the sun's movement. The 25-story towers were designed by AHR (formerly Aedas UK) for the Abu Dhabi Investment Council.

Dynamic facade

The mashrabiya units reduce solar gain inside the building by up to 50 percent, reducing carbon dioxide (CO_2) emissions by up to 25 percent a year, equivalent to more than a thousand tons of CO_2. Each mashrabiya unit is secured to the building at the point of each triangle with an actuator in the middle opening and closing the mechanism. Computational modeling and manufacturing were essential in the design and construction of the 244 different configurations of mashrabiya unit. Each of the 12,588 aluminum-frame components is unique; no two angles in any triangular piece are the same.

Vernacular design

The mashrabiya has been used for millennia as an effective method for shading, with many designs being highly intricate and sophisticated in their decorative configuration and workmanship.

Geometry

The distinctive geometry of the mashrabiya screen was based on the relationship between the circle and triangle. Each unit is triangular when open, cumulatively forming a series of hexagonal patterns that collectively creates a honeycomb appearance enveloping the building.

Elbphilharmonie

location: *Hamburg, Germany*

architect: *Herzog & de Meuron*

completed: *2017*

Although not a skyscraper by modern standards, the Elbphilharmonie concert hall, designed by Herzog & de Meuron, is an exceptionally innovative structure. It is the tallest building in the historic port city of Hamburg, reaching a height of 354 feet (108 m) by piggy-backing on an old, eight-story warehouse, the Kaispeicher, designed by Kallmorgen & Partners and built in 1963. The soaring crystalline facade that rises above the brick walls of the original building is designed to reflect the changing conditions of the weather and surrounding water of the Elbe River.

Big investment

Large building projects always present a financial risk, but the adaptive reuse of existing buildings can both increase that risk and, if successful, reap rich rewards. Despite its billion-dollar price tag, Herzog & de Meuron's design has become an icon in much the same way as they achieved with their conversion of London's Bankside Power Station into the Tate Modern.

Perfect pitch

The building's perfect acoustic conditions suited to both live classical music and electronic sound systems were created by the world-renowned Japanese acoustician Yasuhisa Toyota. To achieve this, Toyota placed 10,000 gypsum fiber panels around the walls and a huge reflector hung from the ceiling of the main concert hall to deflect the sound waves. Huge steel spring elements buffer the concrete shells of each of the two music halls to ensure they are acoustically autonomous, so that no sound can penetrate into or leak out from either space.

Venues

The huge building contains three concert venues: the 2,150-seater Grand Hall, the 550-seater Recital Hall, and 170-capacity Kaistudios, an educational facility.

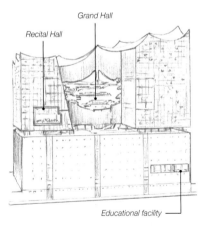

Recital Hall

Grand Hall

Educational facility

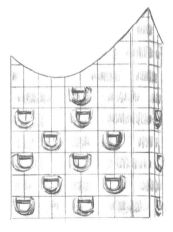

Big roof

The distinctive glass facade, with its curved roofline and 1,000 individually designed curved glass panels, glistens above Hamburg's skyline and deliberately contrasts with the solid rectilinear brick mass of the former warehouse.

La Grande Arche de la Défense

location: *Paris, France*

architects: *Johan Otto von Spreckelsen / Paul Andreu*

completed: *1989*

Located in the new business district of La Défense west of Paris, La Grande Arche is the first tall structure to dominate the Paris skyline since the completion of the Eiffel Tower in 1889 (see page 41). Designed by the Danish architect Johan Otto von Spreckelsen, and completed by the French architect Paul Andreu, the 360-foot-high (110 m) and 348-foot-wide (106 m) structure contains 35 floors of office space. The arch is square in plan and although it is designed to align with the historic "Grand Axe," it is actually offset by six degrees because of the deep foundation piles needed to avoid the complex network of tunnels beneath the site.

Modern monument

Constructed of prestressed concrete faced in glass, granite, and white Carrara marble, the Grande Arche is a modern adaptation of the triumphal arch. It was one of a series of monumental projects, including the Pyramide du Louvre, to commemorate the bicentenary of the French Revolution in 1789, just as the Eiffel Tower commemorated the centenary.

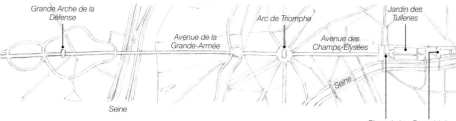

Grande Arche de la Défense

Avenue de la Grande-Armée

Arc de Triomphe

Avenue des Champs-Élysées

Jardin des Tuileries

Seine

Seine

Place de la Concorde

Pyramide/ Musée du Louvre

Grand Axe

La Grande Arche was designed to terminate the east–west axis, known as the "Grand Axe" or "Voie Triomphale" (Triumphal Way), that links the Louvre and La Défense via the Jardin des Tuileries and the Arc de Triomphe de l'Étoile.

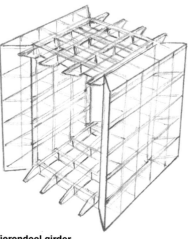

Vierendeel girder

La Grande Arche is essentially two buildings side by side linked top and bottom by a special type of truss, known as a Vierendeel truss, to complete the square section structurally without obstructing the functional spaces inside and outside the building.

The cloud

Hanging in the void at the base of the arch is a plastic tentlike structure secured to the arch by steel cables. Dubbed "the cloud," this is designed to reduce wind resistance and to humanize the monumental proportions of the arch at street level.

F&F Tower

Completed in 2011 and originally called the Revolution Tower, the F&F Tower's distinctive twisting structure was conceived as part of an in-house experiment that happened to be seen by a prospective client seeking an office tower. It consequently became reality. Designed by a local architectural practice, the 797-foot-tall (243 m) reinforced concrete tower rotates around a main concrete core containing services and elevators to create a dynamic helix shape.

location: *Panama City, Panama*

architect: *Pinzón Lozano y Asociados*

completed: *2011*

Limited budget

With a budget of just $50 million, the tower was constructed on a relatively small piece of land (less than 2,400 square yards/ 2,000 m²) in downtown Panama.

Tower with a twist

The design rotates from the 14th floor above the cuboid base, which contains parking spaces. Each story rotates 9 degrees, creating four balconies on the floor below and completing a 360-degree rotation throughout the height of the building.

Emerald facade

The F&F Tower is distinctive not only for its spiraling form but also for its shimmering facade of emerald glass. With advances in glass manufacturing, many modern skyscrapers use glass to provide a distinctive character designed to reflect the changing climatic conditions.

The rotation that forms the helixlike form gives each floor four exterior balconies

The facade is covered with emerald-color mirror tiles

Needle spire

The floor plates reduce in size toward the tower's summit to create a distinctive crown and visual climax that is topped by a tall triangular spire.

CCTV Tower

location: *Beijing, China*

architects: *OMA / ECADI*

completed: *2012*

Structural design
The building is one entire structure fabricated from massive tubular steel sections with no expansion or movement joints. The building's structure comprises 41,882 steel components with a combined weight of 138,000 US tons.

The design of Beijing's CCTV Tower reimagines the comparatively two-dimensional vertical skyscraper by twisting it into six perpendicular masses that form a continuous three-dimensional geometric loop, with the 246-foot (75-m) cantilevered corner appearing to defy gravity. Designed by Office for Metropolitan Architecture in partnership with the East China Architectural Design & Research Institute Co. Ltd. and the engineering firm Arup, the iconic 768-foot-tall (234 m) structure, nicknamed locally "Big Pants," was completed in time for the Beijing 2008 Olympics, but it was not fitted out and completed until three years later. It provides almost 600,000 square yards (500,000 m²) of floorspace.

Configuration (right)

The two towers are 45 and 51 stories respectively and rise at a 6-degree angle. The ten-story base projects from the building in the opposite direction to the cantilevered section, which begins at the 37th floor.

Invisible forces made visible (left)

Sophisticated engineering and computer modeling made this structure possible, reconciling the complex forces that would otherwise topple the building. These invisible forces are made visible on the building's facade through triangulated steel tubes that reflect the areas of structural stress.

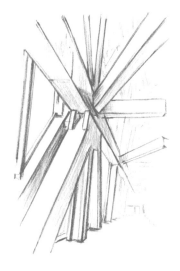

Form follows function

The different elements of the building were designed to house and encourage the integration of the 10,000 staff and the different TV production processes, from the studios in the base section, to Towers 1 and 2, which contain editing suites and news broadcasting respectively, to the offices in the cantilevered top called the Overhang.

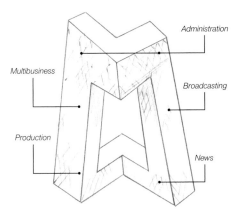

Administration

Multibusiness

Broadcasting

Production

News

Mode Gakuen Cocoon Tower

Inspired by the structure and formal appearance of the cocoon, this 668-foot-tall (204 m) skyscraper was designed to house three educational institutions, making it the second tallest educational building in the world to the Moscow State University (see page 107). The building reimagined the conventional horizontal typology of educational buildings by creating instead a vertical campus for 10,000 students in three educational institutions: the fashion school, Tokyo Mode Gakuen; the IT school, HAL Tokyo; and the medical school, Shuto Ikō. At the base of the tower sit two low-rise auditoria, which can accommodate more than 1,000 guests.

location: *Tokyo, Japan*
architects: *Tange Associates*
completed: *2008*

Environmental design

One of the leading design principles was to minimize the building's environmental impact. The skyscraper is equipped with a cogenerative system that produces up to 40 percent of the building's energy, significantly reducing operating costs and greenhouse gas emissions.

Efficient ellipse

The building's distinctive elliptical body helps to distribute solar gain inside and outside the building, and it reduces wind resistance and downdrafts that can wreak havoc on the dense high-rise landscape. The body's narrowing toward the ground also creates a larger public area at street level.

Complex plan

The basic structure is a conventional concrete service core with surrounding steel frame. Internally, the rooms are arranged according to a complex plan. From the first to the 50th stories, three rectangular classrooms branch out from the core at 120-degree intervals on each level, with the interstitial space occupied by three-story-high lounges providing rest and relaxation.

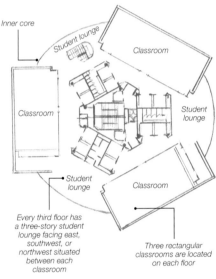

Inner core

Student lounge

Classroom

Classroom

Student lounge

Student lounge

Classroom

Every third floor has a three-story student lounge facing east, southwest, or northwest situated between each classroom

Three rectangular classrooms are located on each floor

Facade design

The distinctive facade is created by the combination of glazing and aluminum cladding to create a lattice effect, similar to the surface of a cocoon.

Elephant Building

location: *Bangkok, Thailand*

architects: *Sumet Jumsai / Ong-ard Satrabhandhu*

completed: *1997*

Symbolism
More formally known as the Chang Building, the cubist elephant is an entirely serious project imbued with a touch of humor.

For centuries, elephants have been revered in Thai culture, so where better to construct the world's tallest elephant-shape structure than in the Thai capital? Designed by a local architect, the 32-story building stands 335 feet (102 m) tall and is 560 feet (171 m) long. The building comprises three bridged towers, two of which are offices and the third residential. The complex also contains a shopping mall, swimming pool, and parking in the basement. The quirky design was conceived by the Thai senator and property magnate Dr. Arun Chaiseri, who graduated in engineering from the University of Illinois.

Eyes and tusks (below)
The different abstracted elements of the elephant's body are not merely aesthetic. The horizontal "tusks" that cantilever from the face contain offices for the management company, the "eyes" are large double-height windows, and the ears are multistoried balconies.

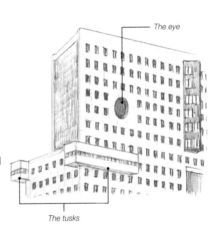

The eye

The tusks

Towering trusses (above)
Two pairs of huge prefabricated steel trusses weighing 117 tons were hoisted into place 33 feet (10 m) above the ground to span the intervening 107 feet (33 m) between the three towers. It forms the horizontal upper section, which contains luxury apartments and a roof garden with swimming pool.

A white elephant?
The white elephant has been revered in Thailand for centuries as a symbol of longevity and trust, and featured on versions of the Siam flag until the early twentieth century. Cultural associations apart, the building is designed to be environmentally and energy conscious with a low heat emitable facade, energy-saving lighting balanced with natural light, a recycled waste water system, and natural ventilation.

Turning Torso

The 623-foot (190-m) anthropomorphic form of the Turning Torso was Scandinavia's first skyscraper, Sweden's tallest residential building, and the world's first twisting tower. The building's dynamic geometric form is derived from the incremental rotation of 1.6 degrees between every wedge-shape floor plate, each of which is independently cantilevered from the main core and supported by the external steel frame. The total rotation is 90 degrees from the base to top. However good the twisting body might look, it proved a headache for the construction teams who could not attach a crane to the side of the building and so had to carry all construction materials through elevators in the core. This core rises vertically and does not twist.

location: *Malmö, Sweden*
architect: *Santiago Calatrava*
completed: *2005*

Figurative form
The shape of the building is derived from Santiago Calatrava's interest in art and classical life drawing. The nine sections can be read as reflecting in abstract form the sections of the human body twisting, contorting, and bracing.

Pentagonal plan

The building's twisting form is produced by a five-side wedge-shape floor plan cantilevered from a circular concrete core. Because each floor cantilevers independently, the loads are contained within the building's core.

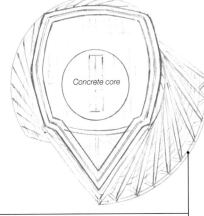

Concrete core

Exoskeleton

Sections (right)

The tower comprises a series of vertically stacked sections, each of which is five stories high. The top seven sections afford the best views and, therefore, accommodate around 150 apartments. The lowest two sections contain offices.

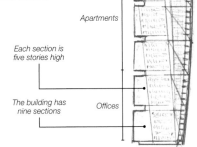

Apartments

Exoskeleton (above)

An external skeleton of diagonal bracing has been added to the triangular "tail" and attached to an exterior spine that runs up the pointed section of the tail for added bracing. The spine carries vertical loads and the exoskeleton provides bracing against wind and natural vibration.

Each section is five stories high

The building has nine sections

Offices

Marina Bay Sands

location: *Singapore*

architects: *Safdie Architects*

completed: *2010*

Feng shui

Tower 1 is designed to lean at 26 degrees, a number that is believed to be favorable according to the principles of feng shui, which also determined the huge 213-foot (65-m) cantilever of the SkyPark.

The urban landscape of the future will be characterized increasingly by a highly complex web of interconnected infrastructures above and below ground. When completed, the $5.7 billion Marina Bay Sands hotel complex containing 2,560 luxury rooms was the largest skyscraper cluster in the world to be joined together at their top on this scale. The 2.47-acre (10,000 m²) SkyPark on the 57th floor was not part of the original proposal for a single skyscraper but was incorporated in the final three-tower design to accommodate certain amenities, such as a 490-foot-long (150 m) infinity pool, an observation deck, restaurants, a jogging track, and a garden.

Wind dampening

Connecting three independent 55-story towers together creates particular engineering challenges to mitigate wind resistance. The profile of the SkyPark's hull was streamlined and contains massive dampeners, including a 5.5-ton dampener in the tip of the cantilever.

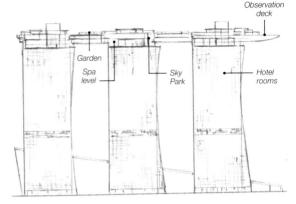

Observation deck

Garden
Spa level

Sky Park

Hotel rooms

Deck of cards (right)

The way in which the opposing facades of the towers appear to bend and lean against one another was inspired by a standing deck of cards. The intervening space between the towers has become the atrium.

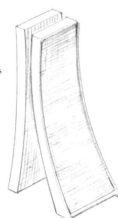

Infinity pools (below)

The three infinity pools on the 57th floor posed a unique engineering challenge to carry the total added weight of water (about 1,650 tons) and to be sure the lip of the pool remains perfectly horizontal; without this, the "infinity" effect would be lost. Consequently, the prefabricated steel pools sit on 500 hydraulic jacks to keep the structure level.

Guangzhou Circle

location: *Guangzhou, China*

architect: *Joseph di Pasquale*

completed: *2013*

Donut or ancient symbol?

The Guangzhou Circle may have a donut-shape but it is designed to represent the traditional jade disk, or Bi, that dates back millennia and symbolizes heaven. Some claim that it was deliberately designed to form the auspicious number 8 when reflected in the water.

In the 21st century, skyscrapers no longer confirm to the conventional vertical typology. Increasingly, architects and engineers empowered by advanced computer-aided technology are able to design tall buildings in all kinds of shapes and sizes. One of the more curious examples is the 453-foot (138-m), 33-story Guangzhou Circle, designed by the Italian architect Joseph di Pasquale, with its 148-foot (45-m) hole through the middle and a garden terrace extending the width of the building on the 30th floor. The design intention was to create a new landmark for Guangzhou and an icon that would be as instantly recognizable as the ideograms used in Chinese writing.

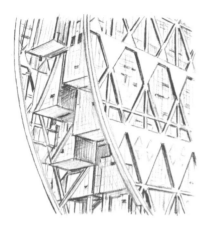

Diagrid (below)

The round form precludes the use of a conventional vertical structure, such as a core in the center or an orthogonal steel frame. Instead, the facade is composed of a series of diagonal steel elements known as a diagrid, which is structurally more efficient than vertical columns.

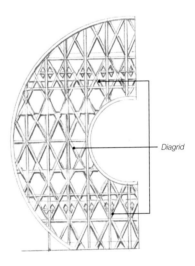

Diagrid

The Circle (above)

The circular appearance is achieved with the huge copper-plate facades at the front and rear, which conceal staggered cuboid volumes that are cantilevered up to 82 feet (25 m) from the building and form its sides.

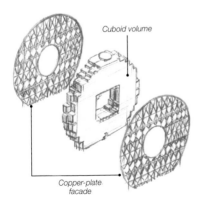

Cuboid volume

Copper-plate facade

East and West

The design not only reflects Chinese symbolism, but also the Renaissance notion of "squaring the circle" (*la quadratura del cerchio*), with the square volumes that form the sides being contained with the circular facades at the front and rear.

MahaNakhon

location: *Bangkok, Thailand*

architects: *Ole Scheeren / Pace Development / David Collins Studio / IBC*

completed: *2016*

Thai pride

MahaNakhon means "great metropolis" in Thai—a skyscraper title intended to reflect the confidence in the future of Bangkok as a global metropolis and of Thailand as a rising economic power.

Completed in 2016, the 77-story MahaNakhon tower is the tallest building in Thailand and adds to the prodigious rise of supertall skyscrapers in Asia in the twenty-first century. The 1,030-foot-tall (314 m) MahaNakhon is the sculptural centerpiece of a mixed-use development that contains hotel and commercial facilities and 209 luxury residential units. The skyscraper's distinctive form is generated by a ribbon of pixelated insertions that dissolve the smooth glass curtain wall of the geometric structure as it spirals around the tower.

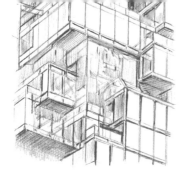

Super structure (below)

The tower's structure comprises a reinforced concrete core containing elevators and services, surrounded by a series of interconnected megacolumns. These are needed to support many of the floor plates, 30 percent of which are in cantilever, meaning they are suspended out from the superstructure.

Pixelated design

The pixelated ribbon is not merely an aesthetic device to draw attention to the tower but also a design solution that provides unique interiors, views, and terraces for the residents of apartments that occupy these sections of the tower.

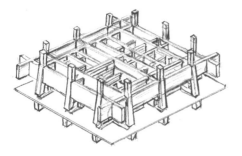

Firm foundation

Bangkok lies on the estuary of the Chao Phraya River, which has soft soil. For skyscrapers to stand on such soil, let alone withstand the typhoons and earthquakes that could strike, massive foundations were sunk deep into the soil. The MahaNakhon has 129 piles driven 213 feet (65 m) deep that are capped on top by a concrete raft more than 28 feet (8.5 m) thick.

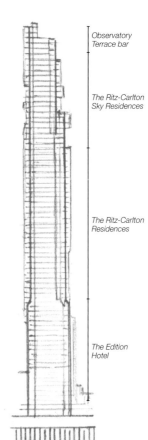

Observatory Terrace bar

The Ritz-Carlton Sky Residences

The Ritz-Carlton Residences

The Edition Hotel

Absolute Towers

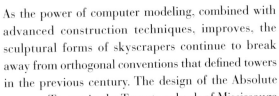

As the power of computer modeling, combined with advanced construction techniques, improves, the sculptural forms of skyscrapers continue to break away from orthogonal conventions that defined towers in the previous century. The design of the Absolute Towers in the Toronto suburb of Mississauga perfectly reflects this transition, creating complex curvaceous forms that embrace a different future for our cityscapes, from their appearance to the lifestyles they sustain. The twin towers are 50 and 56 stories and 589 and 529 feet (180 and 161 m) tall respectively.

location: *Toronto, Canada*
architect: *MAD Architects*
completed: *2012*

Efficient design principle

The organic design aspires to promote a new kind of urban living, more connected to nature, that goes beyond energy saving by improved technology, materials, insulation, and design features. Its success is yet to be tested, but certainly such curvilinear forms are more efficient at reducing wind resistance and so require fewer materials, which in the construction industry account for a significant proportion of global greenhouse gases.

Twisting shape (above)
There is an integral relationship
between the floor plan and achieving
the towers' curvaceous body. Each
floor is an ellipse that differs slightly
in its geometry and rotates around
an axis at the center.

Structural solution (below)
The towers' complex form is generated
from a surprisingly simple structural
solution. A reinforced concrete core is
surrounded by a grid of load-bearing
concrete walls that extend and retract
according to the profile of the exterior
wall at that level.

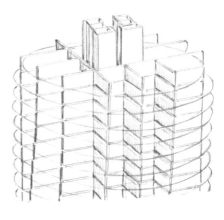

Creating diversity (left)
The shapely forms are not merely aesthetic,
but generate interiors that are unique,
creating diverse spaces inside the buildings
as well as unique terraces and views
outside. Each floor has a continuous
balcony that encircles the entire building
for shading from the summer sun and
capturing the winter sun.

Sheraton Huzhou Hot Spring Resort

location: *Huzhou, China*
architect: *Ma Yansong*
completed: *2013*

The proliferation of bizarrely shaped skyscrapers in the twenty-first century has drawn awe and criticism in equal measure, with the Chinese Premier, Xi Jinping, calling for "No more weird buildings" in 2014. However, such protestations came after the completion of structures such as the 335-foot-tall (102 m) horseshoe-shape Sheraton Huzhou Hot Spring Resort. The building's distinctive shape forms a complete oval—there are 27 stories above ground as well as another two stories below.

Local context
Situated on the edge of the culturally revered and naturally exquisite landscape of Lake Tai (Taihu), this skyscraper's distinctive form has been designed to respect and complement its surroundings. The graceful arc is intended to represent the harmonious relationship between humans and nature, which is accentuated by the building's reflection in the water.

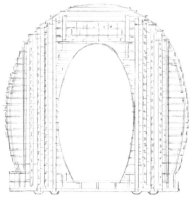

Complex structure (left)
Each of the building's vertical sides contains a reinforced concrete core on which a steel-frame structure rests and provides additional bracing. The floor plates are supported between the core and the building's exterior, which comprises a metal meshlike structure that provides the rigidity needed to resist seismic activity.

Two in one (right)
The creation of a gravity-defying shape like this employs a relatively simple solution of two towers bridged at their tops to create a rounded profile. The architect, Ma Yansong, claims he was inspired by the famous ancient Chinese bridges depicted in watercolors and still seen in rural villages.

Harmonious proportions (left)
Although the building is not tall by the standards set by modern skyscrapers, its location on the banks of Lake Tai demand a harmonious relationship with its natural rather than urban surroundings. The skyscraper's proportions are therefore slightly wider (345 feet/105 m) than they are tall (335 feet/102 m).

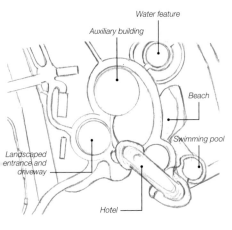

Water feature

Auxiliary building

Beach

Swimming pool

Landscaped
entrance and
driveway

Hotel

MEGA SKYSCRAPERS

The new millennials
Megatall skyscrapers are an entirely new generation of tall buildings that will probably define the city of the future. Their designers push the boundaries of constructional knowledge and technological capabilities, confronting and overcoming some extraordinary challenges that are unique to these buildings.

The present century is witnessing the rise of the megatall, internationally defined as 600 meters, or 1,969 feet. At this height, conventions that govern the construction of merely supertall skyscrapers (above 984 feet/300 meters) are literally thrown to the wind. Megatalls are subjected to such huge wind loads that innovative design solutions are needed to counter these extreme forces. The exterior shape and tapering form of all megatall buildings reflect this unavoidable natural condition, while hidden within are clever devices designed to reduce the building's movement.

Designers of megatall buildings must also contend with ground movement. This might occur slowly in response to the huge pressures created by the building

or suddenly if caused by earthquakes. The design and construction of deep foundations and of the structure above ground are critical in providing the strength and flexibility to ensure the building remains upright.

Another factor unique to the megatall is transportation. The invention of the motorized elevator revolutionized tall building design in the nineteenth century, but in megatall skyscrapers this technology is a constraint. Steel cables can be used to a height of around 1,640 feet, after which their own weight compromises their effectiveness and that of the motors that wind the cable. As technological innovations continue to push the height of the megatall skyscraper, in the future the sky may no longer be the limit of our building.

Taipei 101

location: *Taipei*

architect: *C. Y. Lee & Partners*

completed: *2004*

Water capture

Taipei 101 prides itself on its environmental design, which includes the capturing and recycling of up to one-third its water needs via the roof and facade design. In 2011, when the building was awarded the highest LEED certification, it became the world's largest "green" skyscraper.

From 2004 to 2010, the giant pagoda-like form of Taipei 101 was the world's tallest building, rising 1,667 feet (508 m) into the sky. Located on one of the world's most active earthquake zones, its design is dictated by the need to withstand a once-in-a-millennium earthquake, as well as more frequent typhoons. Eight giant columns, each with a 3-inch-thick (90 cm) steel plate that contains super-strength concrete, rise through the superstructure and reinforce the braced steel core. Steel megatrusses further strengthen the whole structure, which required more than 1,118 miles (1,800 km) of welding lines to weld all the components together.

Steel ball

To prevent the tower from swaying in typhoons and earthquakes, two large steel balls in the spire and a massive (727-ton) steel ball hanging from the 92nd to the 87th floors, act as dampers and swing like pendulums to counter movement.

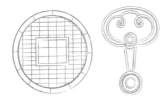

Local identity

The design of Taipei 101 is replete with detailing derived from Chinese tradition. Above the tapered 27-story base, the building rises in eight sections, each with eight stories (the number eight being auspicious to the Chinese). The profile of these sections recalls the pagodas of ancient China as well as resembling upturned petals, which are also a propitious symbol.

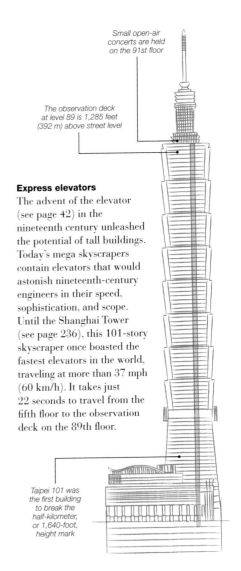

Small open-air concerts are held on the 91st floor

The observation deck at level 89 is 1,285 feet (392 m) above street level

Express elevators

The advent of the elevator (see page 42) in the nineteenth century unleashed the potential of tall buildings. Today's mega skyscrapers contain elevators that would astonish nineteenth-century engineers in their speed, sophistication, and scope. Until the Shanghai Tower (see page 236), this 101-story skyscraper once boasted the fastest elevators in the world, traveling at more than 37 mph (60 km/h). It takes just 22 seconds to travel from the fifth floor to the observation deck on the 89th floor.

Taipei 101 was the first building to break the half-kilometer, or 1,640-foot, height mark

MEGA SKYSCRAPERS

Guangzhou CTF
Finance Center

location: *Guanzhou, China*

architect: *Kohn Pedersen Fox*

completed: *2016*

The 21st century has seen a rapid increase in the design and construction of mega skyscrapers. In China's southern city of Guangzhou (formerly Canton), the new CTF (Chow Tai Fook) Finance Center designed by Kohn Pedersen Fox Associates and completed in 2016 stands 1,739 feet (530 m) tall with 111 stories above ground. Nonetheless, it is still only the third tallest building in China. The tower, which rises from an eight-story podium, is part of a mixed-use development containing hotel, residential, office, commercial, and leisure facilities.

Simplicity

The principal design feature of this skyscraper's design conveys a simplicity that shuns the recent trend for weird and wonderful shapes. Here, the sides are sheer vertical walls that rise uninterrupted from base to top on one side and on the others step back to demarcate the change in function and create a staggered profile that provides roof gardens at each setback.

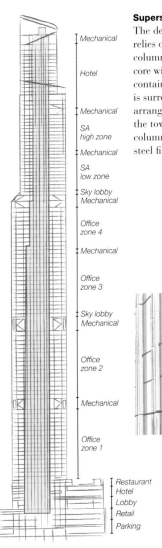

Mechanical

Hotel

Mechanical

SA
high zone

Mechanical

SA
low zone

Sky lobby
Mechanical

Office
zone 4

Mechanical

Office
zone 3

Sky lobby
Mechanical

Office
zone 2

Mechanical

Office
zone 1

Restaurant
Hotel
Lobby
Retail
Parking

Superstructure (below)

The design of this mega skyscraper
relies on the conventional core and
column approach, where a concrete
core with 105-foot (62-m) sides, which
contains elevators and other services,
is surrounded by eight megacolumns
arranged in pairs on each side of
the tower. These superstrength
columns are fabricated from
steel filled with concrete.

*Core and column design
resists movement and
allows for more window
openings on the sides*

Concrete core

*Superstrength
columns
(two per side)*

Window details (left)

Vertical terra-cotta mullions
have been incorporated
into the facade to shield
the windows from the sun,
thereby reducing the
building's energy
requirements for air-
conditioning.

Mixed use (left)

A 251-room hotel occupies the top 16 floors, with 24
floors of 355 apartments below that, and offices from
the 66th floor down to the seventh floor. The podium
and basement contain a variety of commercial and
entertainment facilities.

One World Trade Center

Environmental credentials

This skyscraper uses less electricity and consumes about 30 percent less water than the local building codes demand; 95 percent of the steel in the frame that surrounds the reinforced concrete core is recycled. The "green concrete" is made from industrial waste and by-products of coal plants and ore processing.

Few skyscrapers carry such symbolic significance as New York's One World Trade Center. Constructed on the northwest corner of the site formerly occupied by the Twin Towers destroyed by terrorists on September 11, 2001 (see page 164), One World Trade Center rises 1,776 feet (541 m) over the New York skyline and overlooks the National September 11 Memorial at its base. The 94-story tower rises from a 187-foot-tall (57 m) reinforced concrete podium and twists by 45 degrees from base to top.

location: *New York, USA*

architect: *Skidmore, Owings & Merrill*

completed: *2014*

Symbolism (right)
The design of the building is steeped in symbolism. The height of the prominent spire at 1,776 feet is a reference to the year of the Declaration of Independence, while the height of the building's body is exactly that of the former World Trade Center towers.

A new footprint
The building rises from a square footprint identical in size to the original twin towers and rises to form a square top that is angled at 45 degrees to the base. The sides of each square correspond with the corner of the adjacent pair, creating eight giant isosceles triangles that form a perfect octagon at the midpoint.

Special skin
The building's distinctive skin is made of stainless steel around the podium and specially designed reinforced glass that, unlike any other skyscraper in the world, extends the full floor-to-ceiling height without separating mullions.

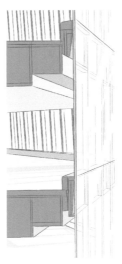

Lotte World Tower

Rising 1,820 feet (555 m), the tapered profile of the Lotte World Tower is almost twice the height of the second tallest building in Seoul. With 123 floors above ground and 6 below, the sleek exterior starkly contrasts Seoul's mountain backdrop. One of the tower's two vertical seams that extends the full height of the structure is oriented toward the city's old historic center. A key aspect of the design brief was elegance of form—the building was to be an architectural jewel gracing Seoul's skyline. The exterior cladding on its slender form presents a light-tone silver glass accented by white lacquered metal.

location: *Seoul, South Korea*
architect: *Kohn Pedersen Fox Associates*
completed: *2017*

Firm foundations

More than 4,630 tons of high-caliber steel and 88,000 tons of concrete (eight times the weight of the Eiffel Tower) were used in the construction of the building's foundations to keep it rooted firmly to the ground in the event of hurricane winds and earthquakes measuring 9 on the Richter scale (the standard for such buildings tested in computer and scale modeling).

Diverse functions (right)

This mixed-use development is designed to be a vertical city and, therefore, contains a wider range of different functions than most high-rise buildings, catering to the visiting public as well as those who occupy apartments and offices in the tower. These functions include an aquarium, an observation deck, restaurants, a luxury hotel, movie theater, jazz bar, children's park, and a cultural center.

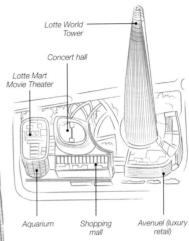

Lotte World Tower

Concert hall

Lotte Mart Movie Theater

Aquarium

Shopping mall

Avenuel (luxury retail)

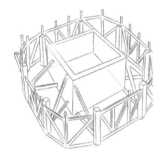

Outriggers

The glass and metal-clad superstructure is comparatively conventional, with a reinforced concrete core surrounded by eight superstrength columns. These carry the building's mass, while outriggers and trusses distributed evenly throughout the building's height provide lateral support and structural stability.

Urban density

Skyscrapers are often accused of failing to achieve the density of low-rise urban typologies due to the considerable space at their base required to make them compatible with the existing urban landscape. To overcome this issue, the Lotte World Tower comprises a series of structures at its base, including a podium that contains as much internal area as the tower itself, thereby maximizing the site's density. The podium houses a 10-story shopping mall, a finance center, medical center, a gym, and an art gallery.

Ping An Finance Center

location: *Shenzhen, China*

architect: *Kohn Pedersen Fox Associates*

completed: *2017*

Flight height

Although officially a meter, or about 3 feet, short of earning the title of a mega skyscraper, the Ping An was intended to be crowned with a 197-foot-tall (60 m) spire, but that was canceled in 2015 due to concerns it might affect the flight paths into Hong Kong Airport.

In 1997, as part of China's creation of special economic zones in its southeastern provinces of Guangdong and Fujian, a new city was being planned and built, just across the border from Hong Kong. Shenzen has grown from a small settlement in the early 1980s to become a huge metropolis—its population is now 50 percent larger than that of London—boasting so many skyscrapers it is difficult to distinguish among the crowd. However, at 1,965 feet (599 m) tall, the 115-story Ping An Finance Center reflects the trend for these landmark structures to be hypertall, hyperconnected, and hyperdense.

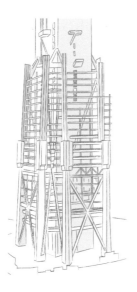

Stainless-steel panels
serve as a protective
lightning conductor

Wind resistance

The mega skyscraper's tapered
body reduces wind resistance by
up to 40 percent, compared with the
conventional vertical facade, which
reduces the material needed to achieve
the required strength of the building
in a typhoon zone.

Supercolumns

The tower's structure,
like that of many mega
skyscrapers, comprises a
large reinforced concrete
core surrounded by eight
huge columns that rise to
the top of the building in
pairs on each side and
are braced by diagonal
columns visible from
the exterior. Such huge
vertical columns are often
contained within the glass
curtain wall, but here they
protrude beyond the wall
to evoke the massive
buttresses that supported
the towering exterior walls
of ancient cathedrals.

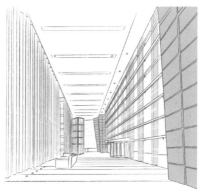

Lightweight facade

The exterior comprises a glass curtain
wall and the largest stainless-steel
facade in the world. With a total weight
of 1,874 tons, the stainless-steel panels
were chosen for their corrosion resistance
in Shenzhen's salty coastal location.

Makkah Royal Clock Tower

location: *Mecca, Saudi Arabia*

architects: *Mahmoud Bodo Rasch / Dar Al-Handasah Architects*

completed: *2011*

This monumental clocktower, which houses a five-star hotel, is the tallest among seven skyscraper hotels that form the Abraj Al-Bait, a state-funded development, part of the King Abdulaziz Endowment Project, which seeks to offer world-class accommodation in the city of Mecca. This huge complex is adjacent to Islam's most sacred site, the Al-Haram Mosque, and provides accommodation for permanent residents and visiting pilgrims attending the Hajj. The clocktower rises above the other symmetrically arranged buildings to a total height of 1,972 feet (601 m), including its 420-foot (128-m) spire topped by a gold crescent, making it the third tallest skyscraper in the world on completion.

Hefty price tag

With a total cost in excess of $15 billion, the Abraj Al-Bait is the most expensive development ever to have been built. Part of this exorbitant cost included the controversial demolition of the former Ottoman Ajyad fortress, which had stood on the hill overlooking Mecca since the late eighteenth century.

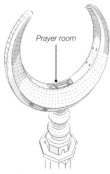

Prayer room

Spire (above)

The spire comprises an eight-story glass-covered base supporting a tapered shaft and a 75-foot (23-m) tall crescent, weighing 38 tons. A small but exclusive prayer room was inserted at the base of the crescent. A light display using 21,000 lamps, which can be seen from a distance of 18 miles (29 km), is projected from the spire at each call to prayer. The crescent itself was manufactured in Dubai and transported to the site in ten parts before being partly assembled and lifted into place in five sections.

Record-breaking clock

The clock faces on the four sides of this tower are the largest in the world, measuring 141 feet (43 m) in diameter. With a roof height of 1,480 feet (451 m), the clock is also the world's tallest architectural clock. Two million LED lights and 98 million glass mosaic pieces adorn the clock faces.

Islamic theme

Access from the complex to formal prayers five times a day is paramount: The clock tower alone has 94 elevators and six escalators to allow for the efficient flow of worshippers. The religious significance of siting the tower a few paces from the Al-Haram Mosque itself and an overall sense of Islamic heritage is respected in the hotel's corporate theme.

The Shanghai Tower

location: *Shanghai, China*

architect: *Gensler*

completed: *2015*

Respectful neighbor

The distinctive rounded triangular floor plan and twisting body reflect the building's position in time and space. The shape of the floor plates is a respectful response to its neighbors, the Jin Mao Tower and the World Financial Center: formerly Shanghai's two tallest buildings.

Shanghai has always embraced modernity, from its early heyday in the glamorous period between the two world wars and now, in the twenty-first century, as China achieves its quest to become a global superpower. Architecture has played a central role in projecting this ambition, from the Beijing Olympics to the redevelopment of Shanghai's former industrial district known as Pudong, which has been completely transformed by a forest of skyscrapers since the 1990s. Tallest among this burgeoning crop is the 2,073-foot (632-m) Shanghai Tower, the tallest building in Asia and second tallest in the world.

Earthquake proof (right)

The skyscraper's spiraling body helps reduce wind loads by nearly 25 percent, which in a typhoon zone is a relief for those living and working inside. The design feature also requires less structural steel and reduces the stresses on the foundations, which, in the absence of bedrock, rely on concrete piles thrust several hundred feet deep into the alluvial mud on which Shanghai barely floats.

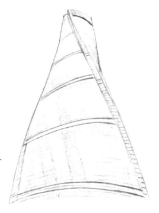

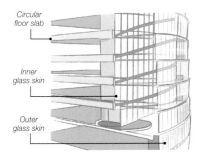

Circular floor slab

Inner glass skin

Outer glass skin

Skyscraper with a twist (left)

The twisting body is said to represent Shanghai's energy, dynamism, and its position on the east bank of the meandering Huangpu River, as well as the sinuous streetscape that was a remnant of poor town planning by the motley bunch of foreign communities that once ran this global metropolis.

Green credentials

China's traditional residential typology is the courtyard house, which in Shanghai was adapted to form the *shikumen* or *lilong* (a type of gated terraced house), which, in turn, has been adapted in the Shanghai Tower in the form of vertical courtyards that provide natural green spaces. The double skin of glass regulates temperatures inside the building and wind turbines built into the facade provide power to the building.

Wuhan Greenland Center

The original design for this megatall skyscraper was intended to reach a height of 2,087 feet (636 m), surpassing the Shanghai Tower (see page 236) and making it the tallest skyscraper in China, the second-tallest building in the world, and the world's tallest building in terms of occupiable floor space. It was to symbolize the growing prosperity of Wuhan, capital of Hubei province and central China's biggest city in population terms, and to provide office space, luxury apartments, and hotel accommodation. However, despite construction starting in 2012, progress on the 126-floor development stalled in 2017 due to airspace regulations. The ultimate height of this prodigious mixed-use structure is uncertain.

location: *Wuhan, China*
architect: *Adrian Smith + Gordon Gill Architecture*
completed: *incomplete*

Environmental features

As with all new buildings, energy-saving features are essential. The Wuhan Greenland Center claims to consume less than half the energy of most skyscrapers, and it also uses graywater recovery systems as well as low-energy lighting and air-conditioning.

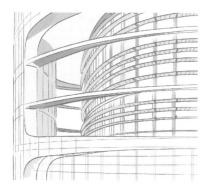

Cladding (left)

The exterior is sheathed in a glass curtain wall that at regular intervals up the building is perforated to provide apertures that allow for air intake and exhaust, reduce wind resistance, and, on a more domestic level, house window-cleaning access and equipment. These "slots" also add a distinctive visual note to the curved, all-glass facade.

Structure/crown

While the basic structure is similar to many megatall skyscrapers in combining supercolumns, a concrete core, and belt trusses for rigidity, the architects created a distinctive design feature from the super-columns that appear to rise up the building's outer wings to form a smooth catenary arch at the apex. Atop this megatall skyscraper is a 200-foot (61-m) crown of steel and glass that encapsulates the philosophy underpinning the overall design. This top section is visually and physically separated from the domed body of the building to improve the structure's performance in the event of typhoon winds and earthquakes.

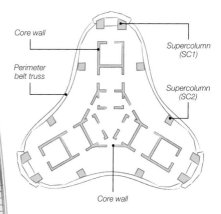

Core wall

Perimeter belt truss

Supercolumn (SC1)

Supercolumn (SC2)

Core wall

Tristar plan

The skyscraper's tapered profile rises from a tristar plan to provide additional stability. It also represents the three cities (Hankou, Hanyang, and Wuchang) and two rivers (the Yangtse and the Han) that define the city of Wuhan.

Burj Khalifa

When the Burj Khalifa was completed, it not only stole the crowns of the world's tallest building from Taipei 101 (see page 224) and the world's tallest structure from the American KVLY-TV mast in Blanchard, North Dakota, it revolutionized the notion of megatall buildings. The Burj Khalifa's height of 2,717 feet (828 m) breaks all records. Even the concrete pumping used to construct this iconic edifice smashed the previous record set by Taipei 101, when liquid concrete was pumped from ground level to a height of 1,972 feet (601 m) at a pressure of 200 bars.

location: *Dubai, UAE*
architects: *Adrian Smith / Skidmore, Owings & Merrill*
completed: *2010*

Elevators
Due to the extreme height and multi-functional use of the internal spaces inside the tower, the Burj Khalifa has no fewer than 57 elevators and 16 separate elevator systems serving office, hotel, service, goods, fire-fighting, residential, and high-speed uses. It also boasts the elevator with the world's longest continuous travel distance of 124 floors and travels 150 miles (241 km) per day.

Spire (right)

The construction of the telescopic 4,409-ton steel spire was completed from within the building, being jacked to a height of 656 feet (200 m) to crown the structure. The spire's design was a deferential statement to traditional Islam and ultra-modernity, recalling the myriad minarets that historically defined the skyline of Islamic cities.

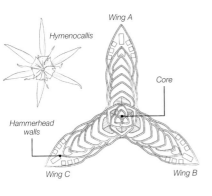

Wing A

Hymenocallis

Core

Hammerhead walls

Wing C

Wing B

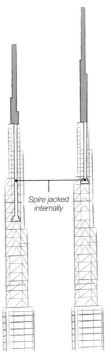

Spire jacked internally

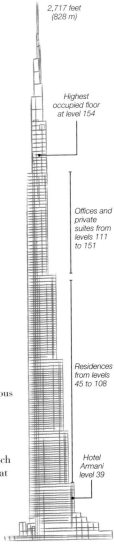

2,717 feet (828 m)

Highest occupied floor at level 154

Offices and private suites from levels 111 to 151

Residences from levels 45 to 108

Hotel Armani level 39

Inspired by nature

Inspired by a desert flower, Hymenocallis, the tristar plan around a main core is set back in 26 spiraled increments as the tower rises. The choice is not solely on aesthetic considerations. Its three wings on a Y-shape base contain a single solid wall with a hammerhead end and perform in the same way as buttresses, thereby providing structural stability, as well as suiting the configuration of apartments.

Mixed use

The building serves various functions, including a mosque, a hotel, and private suites as well as 63 floors of ultraluxury apartments, some of which have swimming pools that pass from the interior to exterior balconies.

Jeddah Tower

location: *Jeddah, Saudi Arabia*

architect: *Adrian Smith + Gordon Gill Architecture*

expected completion: *2021*

With advances in mega skyscraper construction rapidly outpacing previous achievements, the next major milestone is the construction of a kilometer-high, or 3,281-foot-high, skyscraper. Designed by Adrian Smith + Gordon Gill Architecture, the Jeddah Tower attempts to achieve just this when it is completed in 2021. Accommodating 439 apartments, a 200-room hotel, and 167 floors above ground, the world's first kilometer-high building will probably set a benchmark that will be hard to beat. The tristar plan around a concrete core and tapered profile are both a consequence of the practicalities of building so high, providing strength and reducing structural loading caused by the wind respectively.

Materials

Megatall structures, such as the Jeddah Tower, rely on high-performance reinforced concrete to provide stiffness and mass at the building's core. Unlike steel-frame structures, which can sway more easily in the wind, the mass and rigidity of reinforced concrete (or hybrid forms of concrete and steel) prevent the type of flexing that can cause discomfort to occupants.

Structural system (right)

Structurally, the Jeddah Tower has a similar system to that of the Burj Khalifa (see page 240), comprising high-strength reinforced concrete walls, arranged in a tristar plan that are further strengthened by buttressing perpendicular walls, with the spaces between them forming distinct units suited to residential occupancy. Unlike the Burj Khalifa, however, each wing terminates at a different height to create an asymmetrical staggered profile.

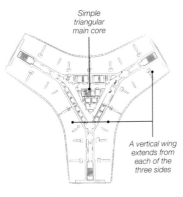

Simple triangular main core

A vertical wing extends from each of the three sides

Sky terrace

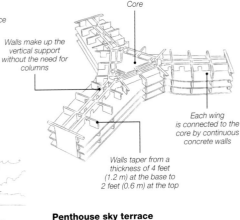

Core

Walls make up the vertical support without the need for columns

Each wing is connected to the core by continuous concrete walls

Walls taper from a thickness of 4 feet (1.2 m) at the base to 2 feet (0.6 m) at the top

Penthouse sky terrace

The highest occupiable floor will house the world's largest and highest penthouse, whose occupants will also enjoy their own private sky terrace on the 157th floor. Originally designed as a helipad, this projecting 98-foot-diameter (30 m) circular disk has been redesigned as the world's highest sky garden for its lucky residents.

Glossary

AUTHORS' NOTE This book acknowledges the vagaries and inconsistencies that are unavoidable in a global survey but every attempt has been made to be consistent. For example, the book uses the term "first floor," instead of the English convention of "ground floor," to denote the street level story of a building. In addition, building heights have been calculated according to their uppermost structural element, such as antennae, although these can be subject to change.

ANTIQUITY of the ancient world, prior to the early one hundreds Common Era.

ARCADE a row of arches.

ARCH a curved opening.

ART DECO an architectural style typical of the 1920s and 30s, borrowing from Egyptian decorative motifs with highly stylized and geometric forms.

ARABESQUE ornate and intricate decorative style either derived from or imitating Saracenic, or Islamic, origins.

ATRIUM an open- or a glazed-roof entrance hall or central court. It usually occupies the full height of the building.

BAFFLE an artificial obstruction for checking or deflecting the flow of sound.

BALCONY a platform protruding from the face of a wall.

BAROQUE a flamboyant and spectacular European style of architecture of the seventeenth and eighteenth centuries that was characterized by **CLASSICAL** elements, but disregarded **RENAISSANCE** formal rules.

BARREL VAULT the simplest type of vault; semi-circular in section.

BASE the lower part of a column.

BEAM a horizontal structural support.

BEAUX-ARTS of or relating to the school of design developed in Paris at the École des Beaux-Arts. Characterized by Classical forms, rich ornamentation, symmetry, and grand scale.

BRACE a diagonal support linking a series of uprights.

BRISE SOLEIL French for "sun breaker", a fixed exterior blind that prevents solar gain within a building.

BROKEN PEDIMENT see **PEDIMENT**

BRUTALISM from the French *béton brut* meaning "rough concrete," a style emerging in the twentieth century characterized by exposed, unfinished materials and strong formal expression

BUTTRESS an external support built to steady a structure by opposing its outward thrusts; especially a projecting support built into or against an external masonry wall. See also **FLYING BUTTRESS**.

CAISSON a hollow chamber assembled in water and filled with soil, rubble, or concrete to construct a pier for a bridge.

CANTILEVER an overhanging projection with no support on its outside edge.

CAPITAL the top of a column.

CARTOUCHE a rounded, convex surface, usually surrounded with carved ornamental scrollwork and painted or low-relief decoration.

CASEMENT WINDOW a window with hinged panes.

CEMENT a lime-based paste that binds together and sets hard; it is used in mortar and concrete, and as render.

CLADDING an exterior covering.

CLASSICAL architecture originally pertaining to the ancient Greek and Roman periods. First codified by the Roman Vitruvius (ca. 80–70 BCE –ca. 15 BCE). Later, designs that strictly followed the Classical ideals laid down in a ten-volume work written in 30–15 BCE, subsequently recovered in the **RENAISSANCE**. See also **NEOCLASSICAL**.

COLONNADE a row of columns.

COLUMN a vertical member or shaft, usually freestanding, often circular or polygonal in plan.

CONCRETE a mixture of cement and aggregate (sand and stones) that dries very hard, and is used as a building material.

CORINTHIAN one of the Classical Orders of Athenian derivation and characterized by floral motifs adorning the capital (see **CAPITAL**) and fluted columns.

CORNICE a prominent, continuous, horizontally projecting molding surmounting a wall or other construction, or dividing it horizontally for compositional purposes.

CRENELLATED furnished with crenellations, in the manner of a battlement.

CRUCIFORM cross-shape.

CUPOLA a small decorative form of dome.

CURTAIN WALL a thin, non-structural wall in front of a structural frame.

EAVES the part of a roof that projects beyond the wall.

ELEVATION any of the vertical faces of a building, internal or external.

EXPRESSIONISM a style of architecture popular in northern Europe in the early twentieth century that emphasized expressive structure and abstract sculptural forms.

FACADE an external face of a building— also called an **ELEVATION**.

FLYING BUTTRESS a stone pier, separated from an outer wall but attached by an arch, resisting the force of the ceiling load, where it is most efficient.

FRAMING a structural skeleton, typically in wood or metal.

FRIEZE a decorative horizontal band on an outside wall, often bearing lettering, sculpture, etc.

FRESCO a painting made with pigment applied directly into wet plaster.

FUTURISM an architectural movement of the early- to mid-twentieth century, one that violently rejected historical styles in favor of technological, material, and formal innovations.

GABLE the flat, pointed, end wall of a pitched roof.

GALLERY an internal passage, usually open on one side.

GIANT ORDER an arch, column, or colonnade encompassing two or more stories.

GIRDER the main horizontal support of a structure, which supports smaller beams. Usually made of iron or steel.

GLAZED made of glass; glossy.

GLAZING BAR see **MUNTIN**

GOTHIC European architectural style of ca. 1150–ca.1500, particularly of ecclesiastical buildings. Characterized by pointed arches, ribbed vaulting, and flying buttresses. See also **GOTHIC REVIVAL**.

GOTHIC REVIVAL a Gothic-inspired style of the late eighteenth and nineteeth centuries.

GREEK the style current in ancient Greece from the seventh to the second centuries BCE. See also **GREEK REVIVAL**.

GREEK REVIVAL a late eighteenth- and early nineteenth-century style, drawing on ancient Greek examples.

HAMMERBEAM a short roof timber cantilevered out to carry an upright.

I-BEAM a beam with the cross-section resembling the capitalized letter "I."

HIPPED ROOF a roof that is pitched at the ends as well as the sides.

INFILL material used to fill spaces between the components of a framework.

INTERNATIONAL STYLE a formative Modernist genre typified by orthogonal buildings, characterized by the modern use of concrete and glass and invariably painted white.

JAMB the vertical part of a door or window opening.

JETTY an overhanging upper story.

JOIST a horizontal timber supporting a floor or ceiling.

KEYSTONE the central block locking together an arch.

Glossary

LEED an acronym for "Leadership in Energy and Environmental Design". Developed by the US Green Building Council (USGBC), LEED is an effort to define a national standard for what constitutes "green building."

LIGHT the vertical section of a window.

LINTEL the beam over an opening, supported on jambs or columns.

LOGGIA an open space with a roof supported by a run of columns.

LOUVER a small structure or opening for ventilation.

MASSING the volumetric arrangement or appearance of the basic elements of a building or group of buildings.

MASTABA a type of ancient Egyptian tomb.

MEDIEVAL the Middle Ages, a period in European history ca. 1000–ca. 1500.

METABOLISM a postwar Japanese architectural movement taking inspiration from the natural cycles of life, and associated with the work of Kenzo Tange and his students, among them Kurokawa Kisho.

MEGATALL a moniker used for buildings that are more than 600 meters—that is, about 1,970 feet—tall.

MEZZANINE a gallery floor that is open to or overlooks the floor below.

MODERNISM in architecture, denotes a rejection of historical styles, in favor of formal, technical, and spatial innovations. Still prominent in much twenty-first century architecture. See also **POSTMODERN**.

MODULE a subdivision, visual or structural, in the plan or elevation of a building.

MOLDING a strip with a shaped or decorated surface.

MORTAR a paste made of lime or cement, used in between blocks or bricks.

MOTIF a decorative element, usually repeated.

MULLION a vertical element dividing a window into sections.

MUNTIN a small vertical or horizontal wooden bar holding the panes in a sash window; also called a glazing bar.

NEOCLASSICAL an architectural style based on Classical precedents, which was fashionable in the eighteenth and early nineteenth centuries.

ORTHOGONAL intersecting or lying at right angles.

PANELING a decorative wooden or plaster wall covering with areas defined by moldings.

PARAPET the edge of a wall, projecting above roof level.

PEDESTAL the substructure below a column or supporting a statue.

PEDIMENT the gable above a Classical portico; also a gable form used decoratively above doors and windows, including a broken pediment where the apex of the triangle is absent and open.

PITCH the slope of a roof.

PLAN a drawing or horizontal section that shows the arrangement of spaces in a building.

PLASTER finely ground lime or gypsum paste used for interior wall finishings.

PLATE GLASS large sheet glass.

PLINTH a plain projecting support at the bottom of a wall, column or other upright.

PODIUM a low element of construction forming a base for a building.

PORTICO a structure consisting of a roof supported by columns or piers, usually attached to a building as a porch.

POSTMODERN an architectural movement that grew during the second half of the twentieth century, which deliberately turned away from **MODERNISM**, drawing instead on styles from several different periods, often with irony or an element of pastiche.

RAFTER a long, angled roof timber supporting the covering.

RENAISSANCE the revival of Classical forms and learning in Italy during the fifteenth and sixteenth centuries, and during the sixteenth and seventeenth centuries in northern Europe.

RENDER a paste of cement and aggregate (sand or stones) used as a waterproof wall covering; also called stucco.

REVEAL the vertical inner face of an opening.

RIDGE the top edge of a roof.

ROMANESQUE the architectural style prevalent in Europe ca. 1000–1200. Typified by rounded arch forms, barrel vaults, thick walls and piers, and linear stylization, emulating Roman architecture.

ROTUNDA a circular room.

ROUNDEL a small circular frame or motif.

SECTION a drawing of a vertical plane cut through a structure or building.

SETBACK a recession of the upper part of a building from the building line; to lighten the structure or to permit a desired amount of light and air to reach ground level at the foot of the building

SHAFT the central portion of a column, between the base and capital.

SHUTTERS wooden doors used to cover a window.

SKY BRIDGE a connecting space between two buildings, typically at or near the top of a skyscraper.

SKY LOBBY an enclosed space at or near the top of a skyscraper invariably intended as a viewing platform.

SKY TERRACE a terrace, usually open, at or near the top of a skyscraper.

SKY VILLA see **VILLA**.

SOFFIT the underside of an architectural structure, such as an arch.

SPANDREL in a steel-framed building, a panel-like area between the head of a window on one level and the sill of a window immediately above.

STANCHION an upright bar, beam, post, or support.

STEREOTOMY the technique of cutting three-dimensional solids, such as stones or wood, to specified forms and dimensions.

STORY the space between two levels or floors of a building

STRUCTURAL FRAME the construction elements that combine to provide support for the entire building.

STUCCO fine plaster for decorative work, moldings, etc.

STYLIZED abstract or symbolic in depiction.

SURROUND a frame or an architrave.

SUPERTALL a recognized definition of buildings more than 300 meters—that is, about 984 feet—tall.

TENON the projection inserted into a mortise to join two pieces of wood.

TERRA-COTTA Meaning "baked earth," a hard, fired clay brownish-red in color when unglazed. It is used for architectural ornaments and facings, and also for structural units.

TERRACE a row of houses joined together.

TRUSS the main sub-assembly of a long-span structure, such as a bridge or roof.

TURRET a small tower, especially one starting above ground level.

VAULT a curved stone ceiling.

VIERENDEEL TRUSS named after the Belgian engineer Arthur Vierendeel. A type of truss without the usual triangular voids seen in a traditional pin-joint design. Instead, the Vierendeel truss has rectangular openings is rigid jointed.

VESTIBULE a passage, hall, or antechamber between the outer door and the interior parts of a house or building.

VILLA a country house or suburban house. In the context of skyscrapers, a sky villa is a large apartment, typically spanning an entire upper floor of a residential skyscraper.

WING the side part of a building.

Resources

BOOKS

African Modernism: The Architecture of Independence: Ghana, Senegal, Côte d'Ivoire, Kenya, Zambia
MANUEL HERZ; with INGRID SCHRODER, HANS FOCKETYN and JULIA JAMROZIK
(Park Books, 2015)

AIA Guide to Chicago
ALICE SINKEVITCH and LAURIE McGOVERN PETERSEN (eds)
(University of Illinois Press, 3rd edn, 2014)

AIA Guide to New York
NORVAL WHITE and ELLIOT WILLENSKY, with FRAN LEADON
(Oxford University Press, 5th edn, 2010)

The American City: From the Civil War to the New Deal
GIORGIO CIUCCI, FRANCESCO DAL CO, MARIO MANIERI-ELIA, and MANFREDO TAFURI
(Granada, 1980)

The American Skyscraper: Cultural Histories
ROBERTA MOUDRY (ed.)
(Cambridge University Press, 2005)

The Architecture of the Well-Tempered Environment
REYNER BANHAM
(University of Chicago Press, 2nd edn, 1984)

Chicago 1890: The Skyscraper and the Modern City
JOANNA MERWOOD-SALISBURY
(University of Chicago Press, 2009)

The Chicago School of Architecture: A History of Commercial and Public Building in the Chicago Area, 1875–1925
CARL W. CONDIT
(University of Chicago Press, 1964; new edn 1998)

Constructing Chicago
DANIEL BLUESTONE
(Yale University Press, 1991)

Delirious New York: A Retroactive Manifesto for Manhattan
REM KOOLHAAS
(New York: Monacelli Press, 1997)

The Future of the Skyscraper
PHILIP NOBEL et al.
SOM Thinkers Series
(Metropolis Books, 2015)

The Heights, The Anatomy of a Skyscraper
KATE ASCHER
(Penguin, 2013)

Scrapers: A Visual Guide to Extraordinary Buildings
ZACK SCOTT
(Wildfire, 2018)

Skyscraper
DAN CRUICKSHANK
(Head of Zeus, 2018)

Skyscraper: Art and Architecture against Gravity
MICHAEL DARLING and JOANNA SZUPINSKA (Museum of Contemporary Art Chicago, 2012)

Skyscrapers: A History of the World's Most Extraordinary Buildings
ADRIAN SMITH and JUDITH DUPRÉ
(Black Dog, 2013)

Tall Building: Imagining the Skyscraper
SCOTT JOHNSON
(Balcony Press, 2009)

USA: Modern Architectures in History
GWENDOLYN WRIGHT
(Reaktion Books, 2008)

USEFUL WEB SITES

AIA (American Institute of Architects) aia.org

archdaily.com

Council on Tall Buildings and Urban Habitat ctbuh.org

historyofskyscrapers.com

RIBA (Royal Institute of British Architects) architecture.com

skyscrapercenter.com

skyscraperpage.com

thetowerinfo.com

Architects & Practices

MORRIS ADJMI
Scholastic Building (page 176)

DANKMAR ADLER
Chicago Stock Exchange (page 72); Schiller Building (page 70)

ADRIAN SMITH + GORDON GILL ARCHITECTURE
Jeddah Tower (page 242); Wuhan Greenland Center (page 238)

AHR
Al Bahr Towers (page 196)

PLÍNIO BOTELHO DO AMARAL
Altino Arantes Building (page 134)

PEIRCE ANDERSON
Equitable Building (page 80)

PAUL ANDREU
La Grande Arche de la Défense (page 200)

CHARLES ATWOOD
Reliance Building (page 66)

CHARLES BAGE
Ditherington Flax Mill (page 36)

BAIKDOOSAN ARCHITECTS
Ryugyong Hotel (page 118)

BBPR
Torre Velasca (page 102)

JOHN BURGEE
AT&T Building (page 168); PPG Place (page 170)

DANIEL BURNHAM
Flatiron (page 74); Reliance Building (page 66)

WILLIAM KINNIMOND BURTON
Ryōunkaku (page 112)

C. Y. LEE & PARTNERS
85 Sky Tower (page 124); Taipei 101 (page 224)

SANTIAGO CALATRAVA
Turning Torso (page 210)

DAR AL-HANDASAH ARCHITECTS
Makkah Royal Clock Tower (page 234)

DARLING & PEARSON
Commerce Court North (page 126)

DAVID COLLINS STUDIO
MahaNakhon (page 216)

ECADI (EAST CHINA ARCHITECTURAL DESIGN & RESEARCH INSTITUTE)
CTV Tower (page 204)

GUSTAVE EIFFEL
Eiffel Tower (page 40)

HEINZ FENCHEL, THOMAS LEITERSDORF, WILLIAM PEREIRA & MOSHE MAYER
Hôtel Ivoire (page 140)

ERNEST FLAGG
Singer Building (page 76)

FOSTER + PARTNERS
HSBC Headquarters (page 190); 30 St. Mary Axe (page 192)

BRANIMIR GANOVIC
Findeco House (page 142)

GEHRY PARTNERS
Eight Spruce Street (page 178)

GENSLER
Shanghai Tower (page 236)

CASS GILBERT
Woolworth Building (page 78)

BERTRAND GOLDBERG
Marina City (page 160)

MICHAEL GRAVES
Humana Building (page 172)

HERZOG & DE MEURON
Elbphilharmonie (page 198); 56 Leonard Street (page 182)

HOK (HELLMUTH, OBATA & KASSABAUM)
85 Sky Tower (page 124)

HOLABIRD & ROCHE
Monadnock Building (page 64); South Michigan Avenue (page 68)

CHARLES HOLDEN
Senate House (page 98)

RAYMOND HOOD
American Radiator Building (page 82); Daily News Building (page 84); Rockefeller Center (page 90)

JOHN HOWELLS
American Radiator Building (page 82); Daily News Building (page 84)

LÁSZLÓ HUDEC
Park Hotel, Shanghai (page 114)

IBC (INDUSTRIAL BUILDINGS CORPORATION)
MahaNakhon (page 216)

PHILIP JOHNSON
AT&T Building (pages 153, 168); PPG Place (page 170); Seagram Building (page 156)

SUMET JUMSAI
Elephant Building (page 208)

KOHN PEDERSEN FOX ASSOCIATES
Guangzhou CTF Finance Center (page 226); Lotte World Tower (page 230); Ping An Finance Center (page 232)

KISHO KUROKAWA
Nakagin Capsule Tower (page 188)

WILLIAM LEBARON JENNEY
Home Insurance Building (page 60)

LE CORBUSIER
United Nations Building (page 154)

JEAN-MARIE LEGRAND
Nabemba Tower (page 146)

LOUW & LOUW
Mutual Heights (page 136)

MAD ARCHITECTS
Absolute Towers (page 218)

GIUSEPPE MARTINELLI
Martinelli Building (page 128)

LUDWIG MIES VAN DER ROHE
860–880 Lake Shore Drive (page 152); Seagram Building (page 156)

DUŠAN MILENKOVIC
Findeco House (page 142)

MORROW & GORDON
AWA Building & Tower (page 148)

DAVID MUTISO & KARL HENRIK NOSTVIK
Kenyatta International Conference Center (page 144)

OSCAR NIEMEYER
United Nations Building (page 154)

OMA (OFFICE FOR METROPOLITAN ARCHITECTURE)
CCTV Tower (page 204)

PACE DEVELOPMENT
MahaNakhon (page 216

JOSEPH DI PASQUALE
Guangzhou Circle (page 214)

JOSEPH PAXTON
Crystal Palace (page 38)

I. M. PEI
Bank of China Tower (page 116)

CÉSAR PELLI
Petronas Towers (page 120); Wells Fargo/Norwest Center (page 174)

MARCELLO PIACENTINI
Terrazza Martini Tower (page 104)

RENZO PIANO
The Shard (page 100)

PINZÓN LOZANO & ASOCIADOS
F&F Tower (page 202)

ROBERT RUSSELL PRENTICE
Central do Brasil (page 132)

MAHMOUD BODO RASCH
Makkah Royal Clock Tower (page 234)

REINHARD & HOFFMEISTER
Rockefeller Center (page 90)

ROBERTSON, MARKS & MCCREDIE
AWA Building & Tower (page 148)

Index

Index

30 St. Mary Axe, London 192–3
Sánchez, Gregorio 130
Satrabhandhu, Ong-ard 208
Scheeren, Ole 216
Schiller Building (Garrick Theater), Chicago 70–1
Scholastic Building / 557 Broadway, New York 176–7
Schwanzer, Karl 110, 111
Sears Tower (Willis Tower), Chicago 166–7
Segram Building, New York 156–7
Seidler, Harry 150, 151
Senate House, London 98–9
Serlio, Sebastiano 22
setbacks 70, 76, 78, 81, 84, 91
Seven Sisters (Stalinskie Vysotki), Moscow 106–7
Severance, H. Craig 86, 87
Shankland, Edward 66
Shanghai Tower 236–7
Shard, London 100–1
Shebib, Naoum 138
Sheraton Huzhou Hot Spring Resort, Huzhou 220–1
SHoP Architects 184

Shreve, Lamb, & Harmon 88
Simone, Giovanni di 24, 25
Singer Building, New York 76–7
skeleton iron frames, first 60–1
Skidmore, Owings & Merrill (SOM) 122, 158, 162, 166, 229, 240
85 Sky Tower, Kaohsiung 124–5
Smith, Adrian 240
 see also Adrian Smith + Gordon Gill Architecture
Smolderen, Jos 96
Socialist Classicism 107, 108
SOM see Skidmore, Owings & Merrill
18 South Michigan Avenue, Chicago 68–9
Spreckelsen, Johan Otto von 200
sprinklers 44–5
Stalin, Joseph 106, 108, 109
steel frames 54, 60
Stonehenge 10
Sullivan, Louis 68, 70, 71, 72
 see also Adler & Sullivan

T
Taipei 101, Taipei 224–5
Tange Associates 206
Terrazza Martini Tower, Genoa 104–5
Thomas, Walter Aubrey 94
Tianning Temple Pagoda 19
Torre, Luis María de la 130
Torre Velasca, Milan 102–3
Tower of Babel 12–13
Toyota, Yasuhisa 199
Tropical Modenism 143
trussed tubular system 162, 163
Turning Torso, Malmö 210–11
Two Towers, Bologna 26–7
typhoons 117, 122, 225, 239

U
United Nations Building, New York 154–5

V
Van Alen, William 86, 87
Van Averbeke, Emiel 96
Vanhoenacker, Jan 96
ventilation 46–7
Vierendeel truss 183, 201

Vinci & Kenny 73
Viñoly, Rafael 180
Viollet-le-Duc, Eugène 29
Visconti, Giovanni, Duke of Milan 27
visual corridors 55
Vrihat Samrat Yantra 32–3

W
Walker, A. B. 53
Wallis, Barnes 192
Wells Fargo Center, Minneapolis 174
Whitney, George B. 60
Willis Tower, Chicago 166–7
wind resistance 64, 67, 181, 193, 201, 207, 213, 230, 233, 237
 see also typhoons
Wolman, Jerry 162
Woolworth Building, New York 78–9
World Trade Center, New York 164–5
Wren, Sir Christopher 101
Wright, Frank Lloyd 63, 71
Wuhan Greenland Center, Wuhan 238–9

Y
Yamasaki, Minoru 26–7, 164
Yansong, Ma 220, 221
York & Sawyer 126

Z
ziggurats 13, 137
zoning 54–5, 81

ACKNOWLEDGMENTS

Acknowledgments

The publisher would like to thank the following individuals and organizations for their kind permission to reproduce the images in this book. Every effort has been made to acknowledge the pictures, however we apologize if there are any unintentional omissions.

Adrian Smith + Gordon Gill: ©Adrian Smith + Gordon Gill Architecture/Jeddah Economic Company 242

Alamy: Michael Abid 24; AF Archive 57TR; AF Fotografie 13TL; Antiqua Print Gallery 39C; Archivart 12; Artokoloro Quint Lox Limited 39TR; ClassicStock 35; Directphoto.org 168; Everett Collection Inc. 38; Eric Franks 130; David Giral 218; Glasshouse Images 48, 56; Granger Historical Picture Archive 112; Historic Collection 43TL; imageBROKER 74; Images of Africa Photobank 144; Images_USA 170; Jason Langley 198; Jon Arnold Images Ltd 124, 178; Terese Loeb Kreuzer 182; Patti McConville 153, 176; Nathan Willock-VIEW 188; North Wind Picture Archives 42; B. O'Kane 62, 98, 194; Pegaz 78; The Picture Art Collection 41TR; Marek Poplawski 142; The Print Collector 44, 49TL; Prisma by Dukas Presseagentur GmbH 110; Realy Easy Star/Toni Spagone 104; robertharding 192, 226; Philip Scalia 156; Peter Scholey 190; Science History Images 34, 49C, 76; Ian Shepherd 36; Stuart Forster Europe 96; Travelscape Images 92; ukartpics 55BL; Universal Images Group North America LLC 18; View Stock 214; Barry Wakelin 174; Michael Wheatley 46; ZUMA Press, Inc. 184

The British Library: 19BR

Flickr/CC BY-NC-ND 2.0: Nathan Rupert 180; Jeffrey Zeldman 161

Free Library of Philadelphia/James Hardie: 53TL

Getty Images: AFP/Issouf Sanogo 140; Bettmann 31L, 45C, 49BR, 60, 64; Torsten Blackwood 148; Bloomberg 116, 122; Chen Liu/EyeEm 4; Chicago History Museum 51C, 66; Cameron Davidson 86; De Agostini Picture Library 28; DEA/ICAS94 54; Nat Farbman 136; FPG 83CR; Paulo Fridman 128; Richard Geoffrey/EyeEm 8, 255; GraphicaArtis 53C; Jeff Greenberg 52; Bill Heinsohn 89BL; Angelo Hornak 158; Interim Archives 72; Stefan Irvine 114; Keystone/Stringer 51TL; Moment/Naufal MQ 252–3, 256; NurPhoto 32; Claude PAVARD/Gamma-Rapho 146; Picturenow 51BL; The Print Collector 30; George Rose 162, 186; Royal Photographic Society 77C; Science & Society Picture Library 41C; Sino Images 204; Smith Collection/Gado 45TR; Joe Sohm/Visions of America 154; Pawel Toczynski 202; TommL 155; Andrew Watson 150; Dong Wenjie 2; Westend61 210; Bruce Yuanyue Bi 200

GVSHP/NY Times 1922 55TR

Library of Congress, Prints and Photographs Division: 160; /HABS/HAER/HALS 70, 77BL, 81, 88; /Carol M. Highsmith Archive 164, 166; John Margolies Roadside America photograph archive (1972–2008) 57BL

LIFE, Real Estate Number, 1909/A.D. Walker: 53BL

National Archives/NARA: 43BL

New York Public Library Digital Collection: /Lewis Wickes Hine 89TL; /The Miriam and Ira D. Wallach Division of Art, Prints and Photographs 84

Shutterstock: Guenter Albers 14; artistVMG 118; Baloncici 138; Catarina Belova 40; Dmitry Birin 254; Steve Buckley 94; Casper1774 Studio 216; cge2010 26; Andrea Delbo 102; Songquan Deng 58–9; DeymosHR 126; easy camera 212; Elfred 230; Gustavo Frazao 134; GagliardiImages 100; Yusheng Hsu 224; Nattakit Jeerapatmaitree 206; Thomas Kelley 172; Kiev.Victor 10; Susan Law Cain 80; Valerii Lavtushenko 82; Eugene Lu 236; Mikhail Markovskiy 20; gu min 220; Morphart Creation 41BR; Myskina6 106; Oscity 228; PHOTOCREO Michael Bednarek 108; poohris 208; Portelli 7; S–F 240; Adi Sa 22; R Scapinello 50; Abrar Sharif 234; solkafa 196; Barna Tanko 16; Aleksandar Todorovic 132; TTStudio 120; WRlili 232

The University Library, University of Illinois at Urbana-Champaign: 57C

US Patents Office: 47TL

Wikimedia Commons: Jacques Androuet (1576) 29C; John Wilson Carmichael 101BL; Donato Bramante 23TL; Doré's English Bible 13TR; Hugh Ferriss/Dover Publications 85; Internet Archive Book Images 43C; Library of Congress: 73C; George Samuel Meason 39BL; NIST/MesserWoland 165; Marc Rochkind 152; Royal Air Force 1944 21B; David Shankbone 90; Teemu008 68; Eugène Viollet-le-Duc 29TR; Wikimedia Foundation 21C